Earn Their Loyalty

Earn Their Loyalty

Treating Customers and Employees Like People

Robert Brown

Denro Classics

© 2011, 2013, 2019 Robert Brown
All rights reserved
Printed in the United States of America

Requests for permission to use or reproduce material from this book should be directed to books@collwisdom.com

The Four-Part Teaming model is copyright by Rudy F. Williams, Ph.D. H.E.A.T. is copyright by Development Dimensions International

An earlier version was titled *Beyond Satisfied* by bp books ISBN 1-43481-316-9

Published by Denro Classics
11700 Mukilteo Speedway #201 PMB 1084
Mukilteo WA 98275
USA

Cover photo by imageafter

Library of Congress Control Number 2010936549

ISBN   1-45381-018-8
ISBN-13   978-1-4538-1018-7

To Gus, Barker, Sheelagh, Colin, Vincent and all
the others who make the world a warmer place

Also by Robert Brown

The HST Model for Change
Lean Thinking 4.0
The People Side of Lean Thinking
Transparent Management
Mistake-Proofing Leadership (with Rudy F. Williams, Ph.D.)
New Darwinian Laws Every Business Should Know (with Patrick Edmonds)

Simply Bob: Searching for the Essence (a memoir)
Personal Wisdom
My First Ten Days in Heaven (a novel)
Things I Learned from My Wife (a memoir)
Youth Character Building Toolkit
Invivo (a novel)

A Thousand Rounds of Golf
The Golfing Mind
Mayhem at the Open (a novel)
Murder on the Tour (a novel)
The Way of Golf
The Golf Gods

Welcome

To a degree every company treats its employees like objects. They have to, individuals must fit in a pre-designed structure, otherwise groups of people will not and cannot move effectively toward a common goal. However, to the degree that employees are treated like objects, they tend to treat each other like objects and, perhaps worse, treat customers the same way.

The easiest way for leaders to manage workers is to structure their activities. Seemingly, the more control over behavior, the greater the control of outcomes. It is the theme of this book that such control produces inferior results.

Earn Their Loyalty is a story that emphasizes the human element of business. There is a lot of work involved in fostering effective interpersonal behavior, trust is vital, and feedback is an absolute. It's much easier just to make up rules, one size fits all. There are many concepts and tools presented here to enable you to develop your people beyond being rule followers. It is our contention that making the effort to support people, rather than direct them, is the better way.

If you use your new knowledge and skills to enhance relationships, the bottom line won't have to be watched with such diligence, or worried about as much either.

Robert Brown	George Corbett	A. F. McTavish
Seattle	*Orlando*	*Dundee*

Table of Contents

A Meeting on a Train   1

Back in Dundee   10

Hire the Right People   27

A Birthday Party   40

The First C   50

The Second and Third Cs   63

The Fourth C   75

The Search for Accountability   83

If the Formula Fits   94

End the Workday Happy   104

Into the Mire of Management   118

Build a Great Team   126

Personal Mission Statements   136

Virtual Customers   149

A True Service Culture   161

The Train from Dundee   176

Epilogue   184

Note to Managers   190

Index   196

1

A Meeting on a Train

Rain lashed at me sideways as soon as I opened the taxi door. By the time I'd raced into the train station, my hair was plastered to my head and my shoes, socks and pants were soaked. Halfway through my trip to Scotland and six of seven days had been the same, dreary skies, persistent showers and a temperature that never roused itself above six degrees Celsius. I was a long way from Orlando where it was probably ninety-five degrees with the sun as big as a pie plate.

The Dundee train station was like all train stations, a dimly lit cavernous place where sounds echoed for a time before drifting away. Pigeons roosted on rafters high above and strutted on the vast walkways. With my first class Britrail pass handy, I found the platform for the next leg of my journey, Dundee to Inverness, gateway to the Highlands.

I'm a businessman. I can figure solutions for most problems and those I can't solve I work hard enough to overcome. But I sure haven't been much good for what seems like a long time. I had been going through the motions at work. Deep inside I knew there are things more important than someone buying a five-piece dinette set. Although I still did my job pretty well, I didn't care if any of our stores sold much furniture; not a good attitude for a Senior Vice President. Not good for customers. Not good for employees. Not good for me.

The train screeched to a halt at the head of the tracks. The two first-class cars were the old-fashioned ones I had hoped for. I climbed up the steps and found my compartment. After sliding open the wooden door, I hoisted my bags onto the overhead rack and took my seat by the window. This early in the season I might be lucky enough to have the compartment to myself.

Within ten minutes, the train pulled slowly out of the station and back into the rain. No one had come into my compartment except a young man selling snacks. My cup of tea and plastic wrapped block of shortbread sat on the small table under the window. Passing by outside were back gardens of homes framed with stone walls and almost all included a green or light blue wooden shed. As the train gathered speed, the scenery changed from close-by homes to distant rolling hills. I settled into my seat. I was as content as I had been in a long time.

As soon as the sway of the car and the clack of the wheels were in harmony, I could feel the forward pressure of the train slowing down. The village of Hodge was our first stop and I suppose we were there already. Hoping to keep my compartment to myself, I pulled out my newspaper and sprawled along the seat to take up as much room as possible. Soon there were footsteps up and down the corridor, some stopping by the door, but no one opened it. The train lurched forward.

Just as I was about to put the paper down, the door slid open. I didn't look, but I could hear someone closing the door and sitting on the bench opposite mine. I peeked around the paper to see a man dressed in a grey tweed sports coat, white shirt and blue tie. He had a Scot's ruddy complexion and was probably pushing sixty. He wore one of those flat caps that many Scots men wear.

He looked my way and noticed I was looking at him. He smiled, touched a finger to his cap and said, "Morning."

"Morning," I replied and went back behind my paper.

We rode in silence for a while, but eventually we both looked at each other at the same time and had to do introductions.

"Angus McTavish," he said, reaching out his hand. "You're American."

I shook his hand. "Yes. George Corbett from Orlando, Florida."

"It is a pleasure to meet you, Mr. Corbett. Are you enjoying our weather? Must be a lot different than what you get in Florida."

"A lot different. I don't think I've warmed up since I got here."

"Aye. It's a damp cold. Gets into your bones. Are you on

holiday to our small corner of the world?"

"Yeah. Traveling around your wonderful country, mostly by train. I've been to Glasgow and Edinburgh, now I want to see a bit of the Highlands, maybe get over to see some of the islands."

The young man with the snack cart came by again. I bought another cup of tea while my new compartment companion bought a cup of coffee and two bags of "crisps," what they call potato chips over here.

I noticed Angus shaking his head as the kid left. He looked at me. "That lad is a walking symbol for much of what is wrong with business these days. Absolutely no sense of service. Are you a businessman, Mr. Corbett?"

"Please call me George. Yes, I help run a chain of furniture stores throughout the American Southeast. And I agree with you. So much of our business is service and we emphasize that a lot. I suppose half our success is a great product and the other half we owe to great service."

"Ah, there I have to disagree with you, George. Every business, no matter what the business, is fully ninety-five percent service and no more than five percent everything else."

Well, I thought, this could be interesting. Here was a Scot from a small village with unknown qualifications disagreeing with me, the son of a successful business family benefiting from a thousand dinner table seminars. I hold a Cal Tech engineering degree and am the proud owner of a Wharton MBA. I have been very fortunate and I'm proud of what I have done and what I can do, once I put my mind to it again.

"That is a strong conviction, Angus, if I may call you that."

"Of course. We two travelers should be on a first name basis. But at the same time, let me more formally introduce myself." Angus reached into his inside jacket pocket and pulled out a business card case, took one card and handed it to me.

> **A. F. McTavish**
> Human Factors Consultant
> 47 John Street Hodge Dundee
> $4\ Cs \rightarrow LC+LHE = B \rightarrow \infty$

"That lad with the sweets cart," Angus continued. "Did you notice what he did?"

I replied that I didn't notice anything unusual.

"Aye. It escapes the eye."

I recalled that the young man rolled his cart to the door. He slid open the door, said "Sweets" and stood there saying nothing more, assuming what he was doing was obvious and that we would respond if we wanted anything. Which we did. When we told him what we wanted, he turned to the cart, picked out what we asked for, gave it to us and told us how much we owed. When we gave him the money, he said, "Ta" and off he went. I got exactly what I wanted with minimum fuss and bother. Nothing wrong with that as far as I could see.

Angus smiled. "George, my new American friend, everything that lad did is what is wrong with modern day business. We miss what is in front of us a hundred times every day. Paying attention to it would improve everything from meeting a deadline to improving customer satisfaction to having employees beg for more work. That lad's actions, simple as they were, neglected the four cardinal elements of service. And, if you're interested, I can prove it to you. I know you're on holiday, but if you want to stop by my facility, I will show you something I can guarantee will be the highlight of your stay in Scotland."

I pointed to his card. "This formula, is that what you're talking about?"

"Aye. It's all in that."

I smiled. "But you're not going to explain it to me now."

He shook his head. "No, no. It's something that has to be seen. I canna tell it nearly as clearly as I can show it. If you've a mind to see, just come by anytime during the workweek and I'd be glad to show you."

* * *

Angus left the train at the next stop and it wasn't until we were near Inverness that I took another look at the card. There was no phone number on it. On the back was the quote, "We're all walking home together." I wasn't impressed. During my twenty years in business, I'd listened to a million words at dozens and dozens of seminars and meetings. I'd read all the books, all the articles, and countless reports, and I knew that these new idea gurus, especially the ones that promised the most, delivered mostly hot air in the form of catchy phrases and imperious principles. The least useful of all were the inspirational ones. These promoters were palpably sincere, and the message energized everyone for a while, yet the effect on the bottom line was an expense item that would never be recovered. I put the card into my pants pocket intending to throw it away.

I spend five glorious sun-filled days exploring the Highlands, including a great weekend on the Isle of Skye, one of the most beautiful places I have ever been. Florida is essentially an over-cooked pancake moistened by the occasional thunderstorm. By contrast, this part of Scotland was a series of hills and mountains, some snow capped, all ruggedly strewn with rocks, grasses and moss. High cliffs and the deep sea were always nearby. The distant cry of seagulls added a depth to the air, which, for that wonderful week, had puffy white clouds floating in the foreground and deep blue sky beyond.

I had two days left on my vacation and the choice of trains for my return: Take a direct route to Glasgow or a slower passage that would include Hodge. The card was still in my pocket. I liked Angus. He seemed nice enough, and had strong opinions, that could be fun. I was curious to get a look at whatever his formula meant. I like formulas and I really like standardization. I like to know that if I do X, Y is going to result. Yet, it could be a religious thing; his quote on the back of the card could mean I'd be in for a sermon rather than a seminar. Still, maybe this Angus guy knew something, but if he didn't, with my rail pass I could simply hop the next train out of town.

I needed a shaking up. I felt better with some pure Highland air in my lungs and my bones had warmed a bit. Yet I still didn't feel right. I wanted to go back to work and know I was contributing something important.

I spent part of every night in Scotland thinking. Sometimes it was while I was sitting in front of a fire with a warm drink and other times it was while lying in bed in the dim light of early morning. Maybe I had a mild depression. Maybe I was sinking into self-pity or maybe I was simply burned out from too many battles.

In any event, I took a cab to 47 John Street, Hodge, Dundee and knocked on the door.

Notes George made on the plane home.

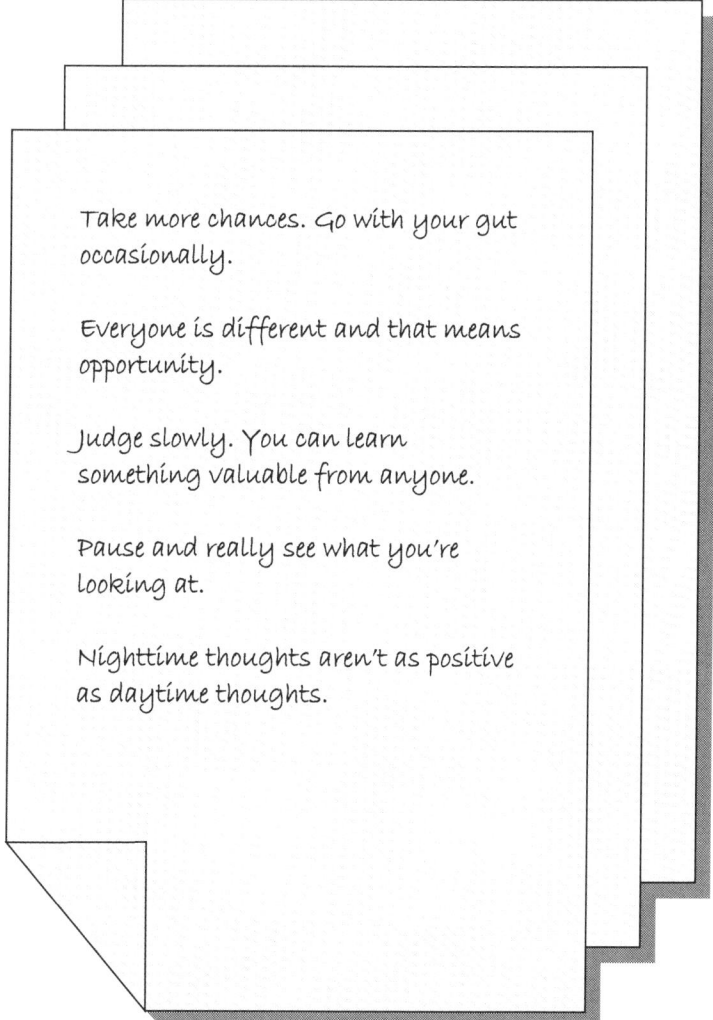

Take more chances. Go with your gut occasionally.

Everyone is different and that means opportunity.

Judge slowly. You can learn something valuable from anyone.

Pause and really see what you're looking at.

Nighttime thoughts aren't as positive as daytime thoughts.

2

Back in Dundee

The building was similar to those around it, a two-story sandstone with large bay windows on either side of the entryway. The other buildings were probably homes and maybe this one was too. Each had a small yard in front separated from the sidewalk and each other by low stone walls. Most of the yards contained a bit of grass and a small flower garden just beginning to bloom. The one I was in was gravel, except for the walkway, which was a series of flat circular stones about two feet in diameter.

I had to knock twice before Angus opened the door. He looked at me, furrowed his brow, and then spread his arms. "George. Welcome. Welcome. Come in."

We entered a small hallway then took a quick left into his

sitting room. Evidently this was his house. "Sit down," he said. "I'm glad you decided to come."

It was a sparsely furnished room to my eye, basically a green and red oriental rug, a brown leather couch and a pair of leather chairs plus a couple of small tables and lamps. I was thinking how a five-hundred-dollar budget at our store could do wonders with the decor. We settled into the leather chairs.

"Did you enjoy the Highlands?"

"Oh, very much. And the Isle of Skye was the highlight so far."

"Good, but you're here now and I promised you that coming to Dundee would be the best part of your holiday, didn't I?"

"Yes, you did."

"You want to learn why all businesses are ninety-five percent service?"

"Yes, and the meaning of the formula and what was meant by the quote on the back of your card. You have made me a curious man, Angus McTavish."

Angus smiled. "You've done yourself a favor." He looked at the clock on the nearby table. "It's nearly half-ten. How much time do you have?"

"Well, I have a little while. Let's see how things go."

"Good. Let me explain some things then show you what you've come to see. Would you like some coffee?"

Once the coffee had been made and Angus was back in the sitting room, he explained what the quote on the back of his card meant. It's something he heard from a friend, Angus said, who heard it from someone else, so he didn't know who said it originally, but it captured the philosophy behind his concept. If you think about life, the history of mankind and all the people in the world, he explained, you realize that we're all the same. We're born, we live our lives as best we can, and then we die. Some of us believe in heaven, going home, as it were. Others don't, but that doesn't matter. We are all the same at the end.

Imagine, if you can, he said, all of your friends gathered together in one place and walking together to another place. You'd enjoy the walk, talking first with one, then another. People would form small groups that would dissolve into other groups. For a moment you might be by yourself, but soon a friend or two would come up to say hello. Your life could be measured by all the people who would walk with you to whatever destination that was your fate. You would have a finite group that would be your travelling companions.

Now, imagine all the groups that could form for all the other people in the world. Friends walking with friends at first, then imagine all these groups massing into one, forming and dissolving as everyone gets to meet and know one another and moves from one place to another. This is what actually happens in our world, Angus said, but few of us see it that way. Our lives are comprised of those who walk with us a while, some for only a few moments, others for a lifetime. And they too, have their own travelling companions. In a grand scale, it's like all of us are walking together in the same direction, connecting and disconnecting with each other, going to whatever that eventual last place is. We're all walking home together. If you can sense this movement and the temporary connecting, you can get a glimpse of the power behind it. Connecting is the concept, he said. That idea led to his research and what he wanted to show me.

I understood the metaphor. It suggested that we can all work together, create win-win situations, and at the very least be nice to one another. Relationships mean a lot in business. Jerks can go a long way, but rarely get to the top or stay anywhere for long. If you think about it, business requires a lot of trust that we are being good to one another even when it may not be evident. I understood this feel-good idea and recognized its importance, but it sounded like what I had heard before. This walking together idea was probably the highlight of Angus' presentation. More philosophy and I was out of there. I had hoped his formula would be something practical. I was putting together an escape plan when his voice broke into my thoughts.

"I see you're pondering what this is all about. If you can entertain at least a little bit the concept that human nature is at the core of running a successful business, I think you'll be amazed at what you have missed all these years. You'll wonder how something so simple has eluded you and most others but at the same time, know exactly why you were oblivious to it and learn how to manage things from now on. You see, all of us walking home together is in your bones. It courses through your veins and is what makes your destiny. It is what gets you out of bed in the morning and why we raise children and why we weep. You and I, George and everyone else in the world are connected in an intimacy that goes beyond our own lifetimes. If life has meaning, that meaning is in how we treat our neighbor and how we spend the precious moments that dwindle with each breath we take. It hurts me, George, to realize how much we value possessions, power, convenience and the like, and how little we value each other. That's why I want you to see what I mean rather than try to describe things."

Inwardly I groaned. I had made a terrible mistake coming here.

"George, you're not familiar with the concepts of Aristotle's Nicomachean Ethics are you?"

"Ah, no." I didn't think it could get much worse, but it just did. The next train was in thirty minutes.

"No reason you would. No one looks at that material anymore. But even twenty-three hundred years ago, Aristotle saw the value of understanding relationships. He talked about love and friendship, and just acts between people, how an honest relationship could overcome any differences. He emphasized how relationships provide significant benefit, with the best relationships providing great but equal..."

"Angus, I'm not much into the psychological realm. All that philosophical meaning of life and such, I don't know. I'm more of a numbers and strategy guy. Maybe I should..."

"All the more you should see this. Come. Let's have a look."

I sighed and let him lead me down the hall toward the back of the house, then up the stairs to the upper level. I guessed I could kill a half hour here as well as anywhere else. We ended up in a large room with a very high ceiling. There was a table in the middle of the floor and a massive five-foot plasma monitor against one of the walls. On the table was what looked like a game console with a joystick and quite a few sets of buttons. A bundle of black, green, yellow and white cables and wires led from the console along the floor and disappeared through a small hole in the wall. We sat on the two folding chairs at the table. I got curious again.

"I've been working on this project for seven years, partly supported with my own money and partly funded through several government schemes. The objective was to create a computer program that could simulate a wide range of human interaction so we could study various models. The military implications are staggering, but my interest is in the individual consequences of these interactions, something that may appeal to you more than you think." Angus nodded toward the wall where all the cables and wires disappeared. "That other room contains the computer hardware that operates the system. It's a Blue Gene/Q prototype that was benchmarked at 104.66 trillion calculations per second or teraflops using the Linpack benchmark. I don't know if that means much to you but currently it's the most powerful system in Britain. I call it 'Hobbes.' It dwarfs another super computer in Reading, England that's used to model weather patterns. I've found that people are much more interesting than isobars and low-pressure cells and much more difficult to predict. Let's have a go." He pushed one of the console buttons and the screen in front of us lit up. "It's voice activated. Say what you'd like to see. Something about customers."

I thought for a moment. I shrugged my shoulders. I'm not very imaginative. "Someone buying furniture."

Instantly the screen showed a woman and a man in a furniture store. It was a typical store. The space was filled with different styles arranged in groupings according to type; living rooms in one area, bedroom furniture in another. The woman looked to be about forty and was dressed in slacks and a sweater. The man was a bit younger and was wearing a sports jacket but no tie.

16 Earn Their Loyalty

"Which do you want to be the customer?"

"The woman."

"What do you want her to be buying?"

"Ah, let's have her buying a recliner for her husband's birthday."

"Do you want the employee to be good or not so good at his job?"

I was beginning to enjoy this. "Not so good at his job. Terrible in fact."

"We have four skill levels which I'll explain later. I'll give him the bottom level." Angus pushed a button that was the lowest in a column of four. The people on the screen began talking.

Woman: "I'd like to see your recliners, please."

Man: Points to his left. "They're over there. I think." He walks off screen.

Woman: Stands with her mouth open and a dazed look on her face. Then she scowls and also walks off screen.

I turned to Angus. "That was quick."

"Aye, but don't think that something akin to that doesn't happen many, many times everyday."

I recalled a recent visit to my doctor where she was late and spent little time with me. "Can you do a doctor and a patient?"

Instead of answering, Angus motioned to the screen. A

young man in a lab coat is in an exam room with an elderly gentleman. "You told the computer what you wanted to see. The patient isn't a woman. The default in this situation is for the doctor and patient to be the same sex, keeps things simpler. What would you like to see?"

I turned to the screen as if talking to it. "Doctor telling the patient of a fatal diagnosis."

"And how good do you want the doctor to be?"

"Let's do terrible again."

Angus moved the joystick on the console and the screen changed to a scene with just the elderly patient sitting on the exam table. Suddenly the exam room door opens and the doctor walks in.

Doctor:	Looking at the chart rather than the patient. "Hello, Mr. Jones. How are you today?"
Patient:	"Fine, doctor. How are you?"
Doctor:	Still looking at the chart, "You're here for your test results and I'm afraid they came back positive."
Patient:	"Positive. That's good, isn't it?"
Doctor:	"No, it's not good. Positive means you have cancer, pretty bad cancer. In fact, you have the worst form and, I'm sorry to say, it's into your organs."

Patient: Looking shocked. "Oh, my."

Doctor: "Yes. In the next few months your organs will begin to shut down and we'll have a hard time treating you." The doctor's pager goes off. He takes it out and looks at it. "I'm afraid I have to make a phone call. Why don't you make an appointment for next week and we'll discuss this then?"

Angus pushes a button on the console and the action stops. "This would continue as long as we wanted it to, but I think you get the picture. The software I developed can handle just about any human interaction you can think of. What I want to show you are the most important elements of..."

"How does the computer know how to respond?"

"The programming is based on the latest research about how humans think and interact. For example, the human brain does not always respond logically, often illogically in fact, but it does employ a finite range of templates to determine how to react in common situations. We use our version of those templates, plus such psychosocial factors as males being more competitive and females being more socially skilled, that sort of thing. The computer-generated response that each person makes in a given interaction is based on somewhere between four and five thousand possibilities. Every person, what we call a unit, has a vocabulary of over 60,000 words. We also have included random events appropriate to the situation. The doctor's pager going off was not something I set up, the computer added it."

"Wow."

"We tested the system by running an interaction, then comparing it to what happens in the real world. Part of the comparison involved interviewing real people we observed to ensure we were collecting valid information. We then extrapolated from that information to similar interactions."

I was impressed. "That was a lot of work."

"Aye, and we're still at it. None of the staff save me are local, but there are over 350 people working on software or gathering real people, real time data."

"And all this is to improve the quality of service in business?"

"Oh, no. No, it's much more than that. My interest is to understand why people do what they do to one another and the impact of interactions. We can test all sorts of interaction models. The military wants to learn the same about interactions and a few things more. You might be shocked at some of the models they want to test, interrogations and the like.

When we were talking on the train, I thought you might be interested in how human interactions can affect your business and maybe return home with a few good ideas. And I would be glad to present them to you.

What we can do is start with a simple situation, like a woman buying a recliner for her husband's birthday and design a model so that her experience creates a loyal customer. You would learn the tremendous difference between that lad on the train and customer service done well. Would that be interesting?"

I already knew the basics and didn't want to go back to

Customer Service 101. "I know how I want our staff to handle customers. Can we give them those skills and design a model that way?"

"Do you have something in mind?"

"At my company, Superior Furniture, we've put together a set of service standards that we expect everyone to follow and we also have scripts for specific situations. We also have what we call, 'Steps for Superior Service.'"

Angus' face seemed to sag. "You have service standards. You have scripts and you have steps for superior service. Tell me about the steps."

"There are four of them. First, be polite and make sure to introduce yourself. Step two is to determine the customer's need. Step three is to meet the need and a bit more. Step four is to say, 'Thank you.'"

"And everyone is supposed to do this."

"Yes, and most do, of course with varying degrees of competence."

"And you mentioned service standards."

"We have ten, each further detailed into four or five specifics. One is to be a service ambassador, number two is that no one leaves the store unhappy, number three is to make every day better than yesterday and yesterday was great, number four is understand and explain, number five is to be a good team member, numb..."

"Great. I have it. And the computer has it. Want to see how it looks on the screen?" Without waiting for an answer, Angus punched three buttons and the screen lit up with the man and the woman in the furniture store.

Man:	"Good morning, Madam. I'm Donald, your sales representative. How may I be of service today?"
Woman:	"I'd like to see your recliners, please."
Man:	"Of course. What kind of recliner are you interested in?"
Woman:	"I'm not sure."
Man:	Pointing toward where the recliners are. "Allow me to show you what we have. I'm sure you'll find something you'll like from our wide selection."

Angus pushed a button that I guessed was the pause button for the action stopped on the screen. "What do you think?"

"Looks great to me," I said.

"I thought you would say that. The computer incorporated your standards quite well and the salesman followed your service steps quite well too, did he not? But, let's have another look." Angus moved the joystick to the left and the image on the screen returned to the woman entering the store. The action began again.

Man:	"Good morning, Madam. I'm Donald, your sales representative. How may I be of service today?"

Woman: "I'd like to see your recliners, please."

Man: "Of course. What kind of recliner are you interested in?"

Angus pushed another button. The action stopped, but the woman's voice could be heard. "Oh, my goodness, another robotic salesman. He'll tell me everything he's supposed to tell me and won't hear a word I say."

I thought I knew what that was, but I had to ask. "What was that?"

Angus smiled. "The system is programmed to generate and express the unit's thoughts in every situation. Quite a powerful advantage in designing a good model, don't you think?"

"So, in every interaction created by the computer, you can stop the action at any time and get into the people's heads?"

"Aye. You see this button?" He pointed to a blue button on the right side of the console. "This stops the action and expresses the thoughts of any person we specify. According to our comparisons, the thoughts the computer generates are accurate to within a .001 probability. That's extraordinarily good." He smiled. "Far better than any weather forecast. Did you expect the woman's response to your service steps? Do you think your sales representative was on his way to create a loyal customer?"

"Actually, I'm surprised, and I guess I'm disappointed too. I would have thought the woman would have been pleased. And you say it's an accurate representation of what people would actually think?"

"It is."

I was a bit put off. I thought our polite scripts would automatically get a positive response from the customer. Why shouldn't they? I wondered if Angus's computer could really be valid. But I had an idea. "If we tried ten different scripts, varying only one word each time, we'd get a different thought each time?"

"If the thoughts were different, yes. But that would be a waste of time. Scripts, for the most part, are a waste of time. Scripts are helpful if the person is stuck and without a clue about what to say. But otherwise, scripts are a crutch for customer service people who should not be customer service people, a crutch for trainers who don't know how to train, a barrier to what should be happening, or a pacifier for executives who want to think their people are doing the right thing in a standardized way."

"Ouch." I had to ask another question. "Can you do high intensity situations like job interviewing, dating, interpersonal conflicts, that sort of thing?"

Angus laughs. "Oh, I can. I could make a fortune taking this to a college campus to teach the young men what they would love to know and the young ladies what they would love to know too. Here, let me show you. Singles bar please."

Immediately the screen shows a young man and a young woman sitting at a busy bar.

Angus gives me a mischievous look. "Why don't we try out a script to see how useful they really are? Ever use a pick-up line on a girl? What would you say?"

"That goes back a long time for me. I was never very good at it. I think I used to say something like, 'What's a fine-looking woman like you doing in a place like this?' But do we have to listen..."

Angus had already pushed some buttons and I heard my line repeated on the screen. He pushed another button, the screen froze, and I heard the woman say, "Oh, spare me. How do I get rid of this jerk so the guy in that gorgeous grey sweater can come over?"

"Okay, Angus, before all my past humiliations are brought forth like the ghosts of singles-bars past, give me the bottom line."

"You have to realize that women in a bar, or anywhere else for that matter, consider a smooth line from a stranger to be the absolute worst way to initiate a conversation. A few good lines work, of course, if the mood is right and the guy is attractive enough, but for the most part, a line is a lie. Women are always pleading for men to just be themselves.

The same idea is true in customer service. Can you see that customer service scripts may be as obnoxious as a pick-up line in a bar?" I nodded my head, but I wasn't totally convinced. "Good. Now, in some ways scripts are fine. They certainly help to create a system-wide norm and a consistent experience for the customer. They are not all bad.

But let's go from the specific to the general. Can we agree that human interactions are complicated, that they are vitally important to business success and that interpersonal interactions are the core of customer service?" Before I could answer, he continued. "And, can we agree that any model that improves these interactions would be of significant benefit? And that employees are also customers of the organization?" He raised his hand with the index finger pointed straight up for emphasis, "And, if we can identify the elements of a positive interaction model then we could greatly enhance customer and employee loyalty at the same time?"

I nodded my head. "Yes, but…"

"Good. Then let's look at creating loyal customers from the beginning."

Notes

> Relationships are the core of everything important.
>
> Bad service is easy to do for some people, almost impossible to do for others.
>
> Behavioral expectations like service standards, can complicate customer service and actually make it worse.
>
> Scripts can be about as effective as a pick-up line in a bar.

3
Hire the Right People

Angus suggested that we take a walk to the nearby park and along the way discuss the first step in creating loyal customers. I still wasn't sure that this computer of his accurately reflected what people thought. Scripts and standards are used at a lot of successful places to ensure quality. How else can you make sure customers are treated the right way unless you define it and make sure everyone does it? But trains departed about every half hour or so for Glasgow so I could always catch the next one and a walk in his neighborhood was a pleasant way to spend an hour in Scotland.

The old stone buildings we passed looked as if they would stand forever. Most of them, Angus said, were over 150 years old, nothing like my neighborhood in Orlando. The sun was out for our walk, but the breeze bit at my cheeks. Once in the park, we sat on a sunlit bench protected from the wind by a high hedge but with a good view of a nearby bowling green. It appeared that a match between competing clubs was in progress, but I wasn't sure because I know nothing about lawn bowling.

Angus pointed to a ladies' team and asked me which player I would hire for a customer service position for one of my furniture stores.

"I don't know. I don't do much hiring anymore, but I suppose I would have to interview them at least. Find out what experience they had."

"Fair enough. Let's say that you had a resume for each one. How would you differentiate them based just on that kind of information?"

"Experience. Successful experience," I added hastily. I was beginning to take the measure of this Angus McTavish. He so smoothly asks questions that appeared simple enough but had significant ramifications.

"Of course." Angus pointed to a woman in a yellow sweater. "Say that one had twice the successful experience of the lady in the green jumper and that's all you knew, except what we can see from here. Which one would you hire if you had to hire right now?"

"The one in the yellow, of course."

"And you'd be wrong."

"I figured you'd say that. What's the catch?"

"Watch them for a moment or two."

So, we watched. What I saw was a team of four women taking turns rolling their balls down the bowling green. When I paid attention to just the one in the yellow sweater, she seemed to be the one who concentrated best, and I think scored the most points for her team. She was probably the quietest of the four. She smiled the least and interacted with her teammates the least. Hmm, I thought. So I directed my attention to the one in green. She moved around the most, sometimes talking with one teammate, then another. She even talked with some of her opponents. One time she put her arm around a competitor after an especially good shot, or at least, what I thought was a good shot. After watching no more than five minutes, I could see many differences but still didn't know how Angus could be so sure who would make the better customer service employee.

"Let me buy you one of the joys of Britain, a double nugget wafer," Angus offered, motioning to a newsagent shop across the street from the park. On the walk back to his house, we licked at a scoop of vanilla ice cream squeezed between two layered wafers, each of which was a sandwich of a thin wafer, marshmallow filling, another wafer, and all of it ringed with chocolate.

"What did you think of the newsagent?"

"Happy lady. She seemed to enjoy what she was doing."

"Aye. Good customer service?"

"Very much."

"Can you picture the lady in the yellow serving us the nugget wafers the same way?"

I thought for a moment. The woman in yellow would be efficient, I was sure of that. But there would be something missing. "Not the same way," I answered. "I think she wouldn't be as friendly."

"The newsagent made buying the ice cream a pleasant experience, didn't she? And the lady in yellow probably would have been more, dare I say, business like."

"Interesting choice of words."

"Thank you. You ken what I'm saying?"

We walked along in silence for a while, finishing our nugget wafers. We had forgotten napkins so both of us licked our fingers clean. Angus suddenly stopped walking and turned to face me.

"This is what I think. You have to hire for service. It can't be trained. Sure, you can do scripts, have all sorts of standards and the like, but you'll never get the quality you want or the quality you need unless you hire it. If you want to rise above the rest, you need to find the right people from the start. The difference between the lady in yellow and the lady in green tells you what to look for. A business should hire for compatible values, certainly and for needed skills. For great customer service you hire for three qualities; energy, caring, and openness. Intelligence and knowledge and experience are all nice, but without the three qualities I think are necessary, the job will not get done. You could hire for just one or two of the qualities and do worse. Do you remember the column of buttons I used when I asked you how skilled you wanted the salesperson to be? The bottom button was for someone without energy, caring or openness, but with anything else we desired, including the expert use of scripts. Each button above the bottom one added one of three qualities I have learned are necessary. Pushing all three gave you the best customer service experience, independent of other factors.

Energy is necessary because it is hard to connect with people all day and really mean it. You can imagine how someone without energy would run out of petrol as the day wore on. Just think how a script would be performed after five or six hours. Energy is also important because the employee has to reach out to the customer, go where they are in a sense. You have to have the energy to be where the customer needs you to be.

Caring is the same way. You may be able to convincingly fake caring about the needs of a customer for a while, though our computer simulations tell us that's unlikely. People see through insincerity almost immediately.

Being open might be the most important, but the data aren't quite clear yet. What we've found is that the person who is open is more able to be connected with the customer. The employee-customer relationship is decidedly two-way, and the customer needs to feel that. The employee is open to listening, discussing, discovering, even at times disagreeing with the customer, all for the customer's benefit. They go on a mini-journey together toward customer satisfaction. That feels good to both, if the employee is open.

Open also means being open to new information that might not be good news. Remember the lady in green? She responded openly when her opponent carried off a difficult shot. She didn't see the outcome from just her own perspective. She responded to the big picture. Say your salesperson has just been told by a couple that they are going elsewhere to buy a chair after he has just shown them every chair in the store. Think of the effect on this couple if the salesperson said with a genuine smile, 'That sounds like the best choice for you. You've looked at what we have and didn't find what you wanted. You gave us a good chance and I hope you'll give us another chance next time you're shopping for furniture.' You don't teach that, it comes from inside. But, if you want to rise above your competition, you channel this energy, this caring, this openness into concise, repeatable interactions between employee and customer. That portion of customer service can be taught." Angus smacks his forehead with the base of his hand. "What am I saying? It not only can be taught, it's what people want to do. Learning how best to care about people is self-perpetuating." With this declaration, Angus turned and began walking alongside me again.

Once we had regained a walking rhythm, I challenged him. I proposed that hiring for intelligence was superior to hiring for personality. Smart people can learn to do a lot of things. He responded by asking me who I'd rather have a repeat dinner with, a good friend or a Nobel Prize winner. A repeat dinner, I thought. That's interesting. A first dinner with a Nobel Prize winner would be a great experience, but twice? They'd have to be more than just intelligent. I could see why I might prefer a good friend for that second sit-down. Loyalty in a customer is the desire to return, just like having dinner a second time with someone you like. "So," I said, "explain how these three characteristics are so definitive of such great customer service that they lead to loyalty."

We were only about halfway back to his house. "Once we're back in the lab, I can show you by example, but it may be useful to chat about the mechanics of customer service during the rest of our walk. Fiona, the newsagent you just met, has been doing the same job for forty years. She owns the shop, personally knows just about everyone who comes through her door and would be mortified if she offended any of her customers, who, for the most part, are also her neighbors. She would be totally daft and a complete business failure if she didn't respond positively to all her customers. The challenge is to figure out how to translate the customer-oriented attitude and perspective of a neighborhood shop owner to the lowliest worker in the organization."

"Okay, Mr. Human Factors Consultant, consult away."

"First, do you agree with the importance of hiring for energy, caring, and openness?"

"I so agree."

"Do you have any idea what should come next, once you've hired for these three characteristics?"

"Not a clue."

"Then I shall walk you through the idea. What do you think newsagent Fiona knows better than your intelligent-well-trained-script-speaking salesman? I'll give you a minute to ponder."

I took the full minute to compare newsagent Fiona to any one of my sales staff. Both knew product. Our people were very well trained and experienced in furniture and I was sure that Fiona was at least equally well versed with every item in her shop. Then it struck me. "Fiona knows her customers and they know her. That's a huge difference."

"Brilliant. Fiona knows near on everyone who walks up to her counter and treats them in a way that demonstrates that. Do you think it would make a difference in sales if the salespeople in your stores knew all the customers who were coming in to look, and they knew the salesperson? Of course, it would, and the customers would come back time after time, just like we do to the newsagent. There is another newsagent five blocks away but going there would be like cheating on our Fiona. A personal relationship of some kind is very powerful. George, I want to ask you a trick question since we've now slipped into a kind of Socratic dialogue; who are your salespeople's customers?"

"People who come through the door who might want to buy furniture." I knew this wasn't going to be a sufficient answer. I just wanted him to get on with explaining his thoughts without me trying to figure everything out.

"Ach, no," he said in the first Scottish guttural I had heard from him. "The definition of a customer is anyone who has an expectation of you while you represent the company. Everyone, and I mean every one, who has expectations of you. Who do you think that includes?"

I shrugged my shoulders. "Everyone."

"Top marks. Everyone who comes through your front door has expectations. Every vendor that provides products or services has expectations. Every manager who makes a decision has expectations. Every employee who shows up for work has expectations. Co-workers have expectations. Everyone in your company has a multitude of customers, including managers who have all the employees as customers. Most of them don't realize that and act accordingly. Many middle managers have technical skills but are clueless when it comes to people. Are you beginning to see the possibility that service could be ninety-five percent of business?" As usual, without waiting for a reply, Angus continued. "So, the first order of business, if you want to stay in business, is to understand who the customers are. The second thing is to figure out what your customers want. Pretty logical isn't it?"

Identify "who" they are then figure out "what" they want.

I liked the simple logic of that.

Angus kept going. "Fiona knows what her customers want. She knows it because she has been on the job for forty years. But times and expectations change and so have her customers over the forty years too. She also knows what her customers want because she listens and observes. And she knows because she asks. She noticed that I regularly bought the magazine *Scottish Walker*. One day she asked if I would like her to put it aside when it came in to ensure I would get a copy every month. Can you think of better marketing and customer service than that? I'd go in when I knew the magazine was due. If it wasn't in yet, I'd probably buy something anyway. There's an important lesson. When it did come in, she'd reach under the counter and give it to me, almost like a gift, while I handed her money. I felt special, yet I was the buyer. No customer can resist that.

Which gets me to the third component. You have to know how to give your customers what they want. Who they are, what they want, and how to give it to them. Every customer buys for value. Some go after the cheapest they can get. Others look for the highest quality to price ratio. A few want only the best and are willing to pay almost any price to get it. You give your customers the value they want."

"We design our stores for that effect," I said. "We don't carry the highest quality, but we don't sell junk. Our stores attract shoppers who are looking for that best quality-price ratio. So, our stores look good, but are a bit crowded by design, like a combination warehouse and specialty store. Then we add the personal touch, although I'm learning not quite as personal as I thought. But our sales staff is trained to allow customers to freely walk around. They don't follow the customers from ten paces in back or spy on them from behind pillars. We also know that having coffee and donuts makes our customers feel special, so we have that at the entrances to all our stores. I think we do a good job at how our customers want to be treated."

"Sounds like you do, for the people who walk through your doors seeking to buy furniture. However, as I said, you have many more customers than that."

"I see where you're headed. If practically everyone is a customer in one sense or another ninety-five percent of business has to be service, right?"

"Right, indeed. Want to know my complete definition of a customer?"

"Let me guess. It's anyone who has anything to do with the business."

"Well done and very close. You're only missing a few of the details. I think a customer is everyone connected to your business that has a need or an expectation that you want to meet."

I thought about the definition for a moment. It did include just about everyone. It was tight and yet comprehensive at the same time.

"However," Angus continued, "the definition is a little loose. It doesn't include potential customers that haven't yet encountered your business and we should take them into account. But the definition clearly allows the business to accept or reject those who for whatever reason don't fit into the company's mission. That is an important distinction."

"You're saying that people wanting to buy something are customers, of course and those that may want to buy something at some point in the future. Then you're saying all employees are customers…"

"Absolutely."

"Suppliers are customers. The board of directors is a customer. The newspaper that prints our ads is a customer."

"Spot on. All of them are customers."

"Because they have a need or an expectation."

"Right, and, they are connected to your business and can thus help or hinder."

We arrived back at 47 John Street. Angus motioned that we should relax in the sitting room to continue our discussion. So far, everything he said made sense. I could see that Superior Furniture's service standards, steps and scripts were like using a pea shooter in a battle against an aircraft carrier. Our focus was almost totally on the person buying furniture and was a very complicated focus at that. If I added them up, we were probably telling our sales staff to remember 50 or 60 different things to enhance customer service. They were all logical things to do, but maybe not functional in the real customer service world. Nobody could remember all of them and nobody was going to do all of them. Angus had some good ideas. But they couldn't be the whole picture. You can't just hire friendly people with high energy who cared about people to make your business work. You need people who can represent the organization. You need people with skills, experience, clear thinking, a lot of things beyond what he was talking about. Even limiting it to customer service, how can he tie just those characteristics to customer satisfaction? And if everyone is a customer to everyone as he was clearly suggesting, how do you measure success?

"Angus, if everyone is a customer, how do you go about ensuring that each customer is satisfied? That seems like a monumental task."

For once, he didn't reply immediately. He pursed his lips and seemed to gaze out the window for a moment. Maybe he didn't have all the answers. Then he leaned forward and looked at me. "George, it is. It is a monumental task. It's monumental in the sense that it has a lot of complicated parts. It's monumental in how much there is to understand. And it's monumental in getting it in operation throughout a system. It certainly is monumental in bottom line benefits. But it isn't monumental in the tools needed to do it. In fact, creating loyal customers and happy employees is as simple as understanding why a child's eyes light up when given a birthday gift. Let's go back up to the lab and I'll show you."

Notes

For great customer service, hire for energy, caring and openness.

A useful definition of a customer is anyone who has an expectation of you while you represent the organization.

You have to know who your customers are, what they want, and how to provide what they want.

As appealing as it may be, you don't have to hire people exactly like you to succeed or make those people act exactly like you either.

4

A Birthday Party

The screen showed a boy about ten holding a wrapped gift in his lap. He was surrounded by family members, all smiling, all eyes on him. However, the image was frozen. Angus slowly pushed at an array of buttons spread across the console. He looked over to me. "I have another surprise for you." He pushed one final button and the scene burst into action. The adults were laughing, the kids pushing and shoving one another. The birthday boy was almost bursting with excitement. "Can I open it now?" he asked, looking up at what must have been his mother. Angus pushed on another button and the action stopped again, this time slightly blurred. We sat quietly together. When I turned to ask him what was happening, all he did was to silently hold up his index finger for me to wait.

Within seconds I was as excited as I have been in years. It was a feeling of anticipation…and joy. An armload of joy. I felt wonderful. I could feel the biggest smile coming over my face. I'm sure my eyes twinkled. Slowly, much slower than how they arrived, the feelings faded. I still felt great, but those almost euphoric emotions had drifted away.

"That George, is another component of our simulation. Feelings. You wouldn't have noticed it, but the colors of the room changed, there was a complex of fragrances that were released, subliminal suggestions were put up on the screen as well as other devices too quick to notice. The result was as close as we can get for you to experience what we have found to be the emotional reactions of the main unit on the screen."

"Simulating thoughts and feelings. That's impressive."

"Aye, but not at the same time and the emotional reaction only for a short duration. We can stimulate that reaction for no more than about seven seconds, but that's all we need anyway. For a complex situation with a series of emotional responses, the system can reset for a new emotion every twenty seconds. Much of that is due to the receiver's, that's you, autonomic nervous system."

"It sure felt like I was a kid having a birthday party."

"Let's watch while he opens his gift." Angus moved the joystick and hit a couple of buttons. The celebration began again. Everyone was focused on the birthday boy. He twisted his head, looking around as if he had to make eye contact with everyone or they would disappear. Angus stopped the action again.

"George, do you think you could describe what the lad is feeling right now in a word or two?" Again, before I could respond, he continued. "But you don't have to. The program does that for us. It takes a situation like this and on command, shows on the screen the primary emotion of the unit we choose, in this case the boy. Here we go. Primary emotion," he said clearly. Immediately the words, "Feels Special" appeared in the middle of the screen in block letters.

"At this point in the party," Angus continued, "the boy is feeling special. This is a wonderful response and very powerful. You might wonder how it is created." I nodded my head for him to continue. So, he did. "All the people around him are important people. The kind of people that can make you feel special, or, just as easily make you feel isolated and miserable. Their attitude and their behavior tell him that these important people, right now, are placing him in the center of their universe. That makes him feel special. If these people were not important to him, he would not have quite this degree of special feeling. But that doesn't mean someone can't feel special from what complete strangers do. Think of a time you stopped your car to let a pedestrian cross the street in front of you and the person made eye contact, smiled, and waved thanks. That kind of thing can make you feel special for a while.

Do you want your customers to feel special? Of course, you do. What else makes the birthday lad feel special? The gift in his lap. He knows that someone, in this case his mother, went out and bought something especially for him, presumably something he's wanted for a while. Your customers have the same anticipation coming into your store. Not to the same degree as a ten-year old perhaps, but anticipation, nonetheless. Let's see what the second feeling is."

Angus adjusts the joystick and pushed a couple more buttons. The action on the screen started up again, and immediately stopped. The word "Hope" appeared on the screen.

I smiled. The kid was obviously hoping the gift he wanted was sitting on his lap. "I don't think too many of my customers come in feeling hope as much as they want to fulfill a need or have their expectations met," I said to Angus. "All the customer service material I have seen talks about meeting customer's needs and expectations. Nobody talks about hope."

"You're right about that. And I wager they talk about internal and external customers too, as if each was a separate species. Have no fear. 'Hope' is the right word and the correct emotion."

"Okay. I'm listening."

"I'll grant you that a customer is meeting a need when buying something and has expectations about the product and service during the process. But don't all those seminars and books and such promote exceeding the needs and expectations? Of course, they do. Do you think that giving them more of what they need and more of what they expect does that? Don't be daft. That's like a customer expecting twenty minutes of free parking and you give them twenty-five. Buy ten ounces and get two extra free? Whoop-de-do. But," here he raised his index finger in the air, "if you respond to their hopes, a deep emotion, you have done your job exceedingly well."

I was beginning to get the picture. Hope is a powerful emotion. It keeps you going when logic says to quit. Hope is why a very ill patient endures the doctor's painful tests and treatments. Hope is why parents allow teenagers to continue living at home. But I couldn't connect such a powerful feeling with the simple act of a customer buying a chair at Superior Furniture.

Angus pointed to the screen. "You see the boy and the hope he feels; all due to the present sitting in his lap. Is it some monumental treasure, something that is one of a kind or worth a king's ransom? Probably not. What instills such a strong feeling in the boy is the significance of the present, what it means to him. I recall hoping for a cricket bat when I was this boy's age and when I got one, a scratched and chipped bat that must have been twenty-years old, I was the happiest laddie in the world. I had high hopes because on prior occasions, my hopes had been met frequently enough that I invested considerable emotional resources in the possible arrival of that cricket bat. Customers do the same.

If this is making some sense to you, I want to continue by adding another couple of ideas of how hope can be understood in the marketplace. Is that fine with you?"

I nodded my head. All my fears had evaporated, and I was learning things I had never thought of before. "So far Angus, this is the highlight of my trip and I can see it only getting better."

Angus blushed. "You are very kind, George. Have you heard of Jan Carlzon who was president of Scandinavian Airline Systems? No? He talked about moments of truth and said that a moment of truth is when a customer has an opportunity to form an impression about an organization. I agree with that. If you think about this, you can easily imagine the dozens of moments of truth each customer has. They can begin with your ad in the newspaper. Go from there to how simple it was to find the store, how convenient parking was, how easy it was to open the front door and so on all the way to how billing was done.

Think about all these moments of truth lined up in sequence making a value stream. Each moment of truth can add value for the customer or take it away. If an early moment of truth is a bad one, it can affect all the others down the line. However, if the moments of truth are all good, hope builds, and the customer is immensely satisfied. Another fellow, your American, ah, what's his name, he wrote *Discovering the Soul of Service*. I have it, Leonard Berry. He said that service is a promise and reliability is critical. I think this is part of what he meant.

Think of a customer who developed high hopes of your store because during the first visit, every moment of truth was wonderfully met. Do you think hope would be high the second visit and higher the third? Fulfilling that developing hope is surely how you create a loyal customer. But there's more."

"Of course, there's more."

Angus touched the joystick on the console. The boy on the screen began ripping open his present. Everyone behind him leaned over to watch. As soon as he spied what was in the box he yelled with glee and raised up both arms. He turned to his mother. "Oh Mum, oh Mum. It's just what I wanted." She kissed him on the cheek. "If it's not exactly right, we can return it for a different one." Angus pushed a button and the action on the screen stopped and the words "grateful" appeared.

Angus turned to me. "In your training program for your sales staff, do you tell your people to thank the customer?"

"Oh, yes," I answered proudly "Whether or not they buy

from us, everyone is supposed to say, 'Thank you for shopping at Superior.' That's a must."

He pointed to the word on the screen. "We're using this lad as a model for wonderful customer service. 'Grateful' in this case means the customer is grateful, not the employee."

"Oh."

"Why would the employee be grateful? Why would the employee say, 'Thank you' with any meaning at all?"

Getting a fat commission was what I thought, but I answered, "Satisfied customer?"

"You understand the contradiction. We want the customer to be eternally grateful for the product or service. Our goal is not for the employee to be eternally grateful that the customer came in. What kind of sincerity is there when you train your people to thank the customer no matter what? Do you suppose customers go home saying to each other, 'That sales person who thanked us for stopping by there was so grateful, we should go back again very soon?' I don't think so. Yet obviously, you do. You train them to say that. That's crazy."

I suppose I could have felt insulted, but I didn't. What Angus was saying made sense. It isn't what we say; it's the emotional response within our customer that is important. What they want is both a product or service and feeling a positive emotion of some sort. Know what those emotions should be and know how to instill those emotions and you're doing the best that can be done. Evidently, Angus believes that feeling special, having hope and feeling grateful is where the action is. I had to sort things out.

"I can understand why feeling special is important. That's as clear as it can be. The idea of hope is a little foggy. Do you really mean hope? And can you explain it a bit more?"

"I can. Hope means looking into the future plus a degree of anxiety about the future. You're not sure, but you hope everything will turn out well. Add this idea to the concept of value. Those who want only the cheapest can compare prices relatively easily and make purchases with little need of hope, only the threat of buyer's remorse if they see a lower price in the next few days. Retailers who market only price don't have to worry much about customer's hopes beyond making sure prices are the lowest available. Customers who look for the best quality-price ratio have a greater level of anxiety and thus, a greater degree of hope. Retailers have to promise the best ratio of quality and price, then deliver. Those who want only the best are the easiest to figure out, although not the easiest to please. It's either-or. Any slip from what they perceive as quality becomes unacceptable. Fail to deliver and their hope is immediately terminated, and they go elsewhere.

Anxiety is a kind of investment, you're concerned but going ahead anyway. So, think of hope as an emotional investment; investment in people and investment in an outcome. In our case, that outcome is a desired product, like a piece of furniture or some sort of service, like seeing the doctor. The greater the investment, which grows over time to become customer loyalty, the better. However, the greater the investment, the higher the possibility of failure. Customer loyalty doesn't come easy. You must earn it, then continue to re-earn it every time there is a moment of truth. Miss one and you might be forgiven. Miss two moments of truth and you're probably toast butter side down."

I was beginning to put all this together. "And being

grateful is the direct result of hope being fulfilled." Then, as the Brits say, the penny dropped. "Oh, I get it. By telling my sales staff to say, 'Thank you for shopping at Superior,' I was diluting the customer's sense of gratefulness. I think. Was I?"

"Right you are. If you are grateful to someone, don't you want them to know it? The idea is to do such a great job that it's the customer who is eager to say, 'thank you.' If the employee dismisses the customer's response or 'steals his thunder' as you say, doesn't that take away from the whole experience?"

"So, if I use the metaphor of a child's birthday party to understand the important elements of customer service, I pretty much have it. For outcome I mean. Loyal customers feel special, like a ten-year old boy at his birthday party, they feel hope and those hopes are fulfilled, and they feel grateful and are appreciative. Does that cover it?"

"That covers it."

"Is this on your business card?"

"Yes and no. 'No,' from the standpoint that what we've been exploring is only defining the outcome we seek; the outcome that makes a customer loyal. We haven't touched much on how to do that. Nor have we looked at how to create loyal staff, which is hugely important in creating loyal customers. But 'yes' in the sense that the LC on the card is for loyal customer. What we can do now is look at where the action is. We should dive into the power of the 4 Cs."

Notes

Do whatever you can to make your customer feel special.

Exceptional customer service is when the customer has high hopes that are then met.

Setting high hopes is important, but you better meet them. The higher the hopes the bigger the stakes.

A customer service value stream is all the moments of truth strung together in sequence from start to finish.

Staff thanking customers is backwards. The customer should be so grateful that employees are thanked.

5

The First C

Angus pushed on the joystick and the screen showed the boy holding his still wrapped gift. "To understand service, let's focus on the mother's thoughts." He pushed more buttons. We heard her voice, "I love this child." Angus turned to me, "That's the first C of the 4 Cs." Then it was the mother's voice again. "I sure did my best to drag out of him what he wanted most." Angus held up two fingers. The mother continued, "I sure hope he likes his gift. I made sure it was exactly what he wanted, but you never know with kids." Angus nodded, "Number three." Then the mother's voice again, "I'll make sure it's exactly what he wanted when things calm down a bit." I raised my finger in the air like Angus had done, "And that's number four," I said.

"Right you are," Angus agreed. "Connecting human-to-human is the first C. Now to explain it. The bond between mother and child has got to be the strongest human relationship. Because of that, there are very few actions a child can commit that would break that bond and a whole lot the mother will sacrifice to keep it. Perhaps the worst human experience is to lose a child."

I began to think about my wife Carol and slipped into my own pool of sadness. But Angus was already into his next mini lecture.

"Those quotes about love; 'love makes the world go 'round, love is a many splendored thing,' point to the immense power of that emotion. Then there is the opposite. Do you know what the opposite feeling of love is?"

"Hate?"

Angus chuckled. "Everyone says that, then most quickly wonder if that is really the case. No, the opposite of love is indifference. And that's where we need to begin the discussion about connecting human-to-human with the customer.

You want to avoid the indifference end of the continuum and move toward love as far as you can. The mother at the birthday party was as far into love as a person can be. Agreed?" I nodded my head. "Then let's look at a customer interaction and see what we can see. Any requests?"

"I'd like to see that lady finally buy a recliner for her husband."

"Brilliant." Angus fiddled with some buttons and the screen lit up with the woman and the younger man in the furniture store.

Man: "Good morning, madam. I'm Donald, your sales representative. How may I be of service today?"

Woman: "I'd like to see your recliners, please."

Man: "Of course. What kind of recliner are you interested in?"

"Remember that one?" Angus asks. "She thought the salesman was a robot."

Angus moved the joystick and hit two buttons. The woman and man were walking among a sea of recliners.

Man: Pointing to a brown leather recliner. "This one is one of our best models. The leather is Spanish." He moves a lever on the chair. "And the mechanism is guaranteed for twenty years." He then moves to another leather recliner. "This one is also Spanish leather and you can see it is a rich buttery color, very nice and it has the same mechanism as the other. It's on sale this week and is a very good buy."

Angus touches the joystick and the action stops. "Want to know what the woman is thinking?"
"Sure."

Angus touches one of his magic buttons.

Woman: "I'm not looking for a leather recliner."

"Ah, hah! There's a lesson for you," Angus shouts. "Now look at this." He pushed two buttons and then the joystick. The screen shows the same man and woman near the front of the store, but this time she is wearing a raincoat that is dripping wet. "Uh, oh," Angus said. "Looks like the computer added a rainstorm to the mix."

Man: "Oh, no, the rain started. Did you have to park very far away?"

Woman: "Not too far."

Man: "May I hang up your coat so it can dry while you shop?"

Woman: "No, that's okay. I came to look at recliners."

Man: "Of course. Let me show you where they are."

"Now, watch this," Angus said from the console.

The man and woman are walking toward the recliner section.

Man:	"Would you like me to show you different models or would you rather explore them on your own?"
Woman:	"Give me a few moments so I can look around."
Man:	Smiles. "Of course."

By now it is almost automatic. The action stops and I hear the woman say, "That was nice." The picture blurs. I know what is coming. Within seconds I have a warm feeling and can't help but smile. The woman must be feeling some of that human-to-human connection. Angus backs up the action.

Man:	"Would you like me to show you different models or would you rather explore them on your own?"

The action stops and the woman's voice says, "I appreciate the option." The picture blurs and I wait to feel her emotion. Nothing. There is no emotional response that I can feel.

"What do you think?" Angus asks.

"I felt her emotional reaction when he agreed to leave her alone. It was quite a positive reaction, but nothing when he asked her what she wanted. I would have thought she would have responded positively to both things."

"Actually, she did. Our computer only responds to significant changes in emotional states. She has had positive experiences so far. Her emotional reaction to having freedom to look around was not new, but certainly added to her experience. The salesman's genuine smile was perceived as a new connection and thus elicited her emotional reaction. It's what some folks call 'delighting' your customer."

"I get it. Connecting is like getting to know someone. You don't do it all at once. You kind of like grow on one another."

"Ah, yes and no. Think about love again. Did you ever fall head over heels?"

I thought about Carol. We'd met in a college psychology class. I was sitting in the back of the room. This girl in the front row turned to hand back some papers and our eyes met. I'd seen her before and knew her name, but I didn't know her. But when our eyes met for the first time, I felt a spark. I made sure to be on the same laboratory team and we started dating pretty quickly. On maybe our third date she asked if I had felt something that time our eyes first met. I said "yes," and she did too. I smiled at Angus, "I fell in love when my eyes first looked into those of the woman I would marry."

"So, you know. How long have you been married?"

"Not long enough. She died two years ago."

Angus' expression immediately changed from jovial to sadness. "Oh, I'm very sorry, George. I shouldn't have…"

"That's all right. I'm learning to cope. That's one reason why I came to Scotland, to think about things, to get over whatever it is I need to get over, to find something new."

"Perhaps we should stop."

"No. This is good. It's what I need. I haven't been so engaged in a long time. I'm learning about business but I'm also applying some of these lessons to me. I haven't been connecting at work. I'm nice enough, I suppose, but I'm really not there. I'd like to get back to discussing connecting human-to-human."

"Fair enough. When I talked about falling in love, my meaning is that it can happen instantaneously. You can connect with someone instantaneously on a less intense level too. What's interesting is that the deep feeling of love often overrides good judgment while a less intense attraction to someone depends on what happens the next few times you are with them. Love has passion, intimacy and commitment powering it, while lesser feelings depend more on positive reinforcement over time." Angus raised his index finger again for emphasis. "The other important factor is that a person can get turned off immediately and that happens more often than he or she falls in love."

"So," I raised my index finger, "you're suggesting that connecting human-to-human should be as far toward the love end of the continuum as possible, that connecting can happen quickly, but that would be rare, that another reaction, repulsion could happen immediately and that could happen more often, and that, for the most part, connecting happens piece by piece over time." I thought for a moment. "And finally, that connecting can be intensified if you can somehow keep adding positive emotional experiences."

Angus nodded his head. "I couldn't have said it any better myself."

"I'm enjoying this, Angus. I truly am. But I do have a concern. Love is a strong word. I understand that you're talking about a continuum from indifference to love and that loyal customers are created by being as far on the love side as possible. But I can't sell love to my employees."

"Do you know about agape love?"

"Heard the term," I answered, "But don't really know what it is."

"Think about friendship, where you want only the highest good for your friend. That's the kind of thing we're talking about."

"Even agape love might be a tough sell."

"Can you sell the experience of a birthday party to your workers? I would hope all of them have had one.'"

"I suppose I could."

"Keep that idea in mind as we explore this further. You agree that connecting is on an emotional level? Without that, you don't have superior service?"

"'Superior service.' Was that..."

"Aye, it was: A deliberate but gentle attempt to mock what you have been calling superior customer service. Forgive me, I couldn't help it. If you want to connect, you have to be authentic, you have to be there, paying attention in the moment. You don't connect by using a script. You don't connect by thinking about a commission. You don't connect without a degree of uncertainty. The more a system tries to control customer-employee interaction, the less chance there is for connecting. There can be connecting, but it is in spite of the scripts and standards and whatnot, in spite of them, not because of them."

"You don't like scripts."

"As I said. If the person is at a loss for what to say, scripts can help. And they are useful in a training or practice session, but mostly to make the learning experience more standardized so it can be improved. Scripts are also useful in large organizations that want the customer's experience to be uniform, consistent. But I think you give up so much for that."

"So, if I want to connect human-to-human with my customer, what do I do?"

Angus got up and went over to a white board. Without speaking, he wrote out:

1. Know when you are entering a Moment of Truth.
2. Decide that this person is the most important person in the world right now and they need your best and you want to give it to them.
3. Decide that your own moments are precious, and you don't want to waste any of them.
4. Decide that your time and their time, your interest and their interest, your values and their values deserve a great outcome—whatever that is.

I grabbed a pen and some paper out of my pocket and began jotting this down as quickly as I could while he was writing. When he finished, he turned and saw what I was doing.

"Stop! Don't write them down. You'll only use them as service standards or something equally ridiculous. No writing, please."

I put my pen and paper back in my pocket. I'd gotten them all down, but he was right. I was thinking about a new set of service standards.

Angus remained standing by the board. "Think about motivation. What motivates your employees to do what they do? Is it internal, external, something you can control?"

A small light went on in my head. "Commission salespeople are motivated by their commission."

"That's exactly right. And as a result, they are going to be further on that continuum toward indifference except where it is motivated by self-interest in the commission. These people are warm and caring until it no longer suits their purpose."

"So, commissions are a bad way to go?"

"Not at all. Think about Fiona, our newsagent. She's basically on commission; she owns the place. So she has all the risk and only gets income if there's money left over after paying the bills. But she cares, she's open, she's energetic. Commissions are bad for the wrong type of worker, if you're interested in creating loyal customers."

"So, the motivation is people. You care about them. You want to know more about them. You want to help them. That's how people are motivated to connect. Sure. Connect human-to-human is exactly that. You are a human connected to the customer as a human. The less extra stuff that interferes with that, the better."

"Now you're getting the idea."

"I would think that the more someone is connected, the more rewarding it is. If I like someone, the more I get to know them, the more there is to like, usually."

"Your American humorist, Will Rogers, once said that if he didn't like somebody, he felt he just had to get to know him better. I agree with that. The idea is to like the customer and want to like them more. Do you want to see this demonstrated on the screen?" Without waiting for my reply, he set things up, turned to the screen and said, "Restaurant, four women customers, male server, please." He turned to me and said, "Sometimes I say please to the computer. I don't know why."

The screen showed four well-dressed women around a crowded restaurant table. From off screen a waiter carrying menus approaches the table.

> Waiter: "Good afternoon," he says in a monotone. Wordlessly he passes out the menus. He stands back a bit holding up an order pad. "Anyone want a drink?"

"Everyone can see that there is no connection there," I said. "It was way too little." Angus pushes a button and the same waiter approaches the table.

> Waiter: "Hey, ladies, I'm Jack Johnson from Wisconsin and I'll be your server this afternoon. You guys look like you're going to be trouble and I love trouble. Let's party hardy. I'm passing out the lunch menus but some of you look like you're more interested in tossing down a few. Everyone who wants some firewater keep sitting. All right, everyone's still sitting. Let's get sloshed."

"And that is too much," I added. "This is like Goldilocks and the Three Bears." Same scene starts again.

Waiter: Waiter approaches and makes eye contact with each customer. "Good afternoon. I'm Jack. Here is the lunch menu." He hands one to each lady while keeping friendly eye contact. "May I take drink orders?"

"And that one is just right? I thought there'd be more to it," I said.

"No need," Angus said. "Connecting varies with the situation. The whole idea is to be genuine in your interaction with the customer. No more, no less. Did you feel connected to Fiona?"

"Yes, absolutely."

"And all she was doing was selling us an ice cream. She liked you. She liked the interaction. And consequently, you liked her, and you liked the interaction. It's a very simple process and the more you try to force it or even guide it, the less likely it is to happen. It's like trying to be someone's friend rather than just being their friend. Does that make sense?"

"Yes, it does. No role playing. No prepared script. No following one size fits all standards. Hire the right people and allow them to be themselves."

Angus cautioned me. "You ken there's a bit more?"

"I know. I know. I'm ready for the second C."

Notes

Customer service cannot exist without Connecting Human-to-Human.

Connecting Human-to-Human should be comfortably to the right side of the indifference-love continuum.

Do what you can to help your customers feel like the guest of honor at a birthday party (in a way that makes sense to them).

Minimize or eliminate everything that impedes Connecting Human-to-Human.

6

The Second and Third Cs

"I have an idea," Angus gestured with his finger in the air. "Would you like to see Fiona again?"

"You want to go back to the newsagent's?"

"No. Watch." Angus pointed to the screen.

I looked and saw Fiona the newsagent standing behind her counter looking at me. "Ask her for a bag of crisps," Angus suggested.

"Ah, hello. May I have a bag of crisps, please?" I said to the image on the screen.

Fiona smiles. "Righto. What kind would you like? We have plain and just about any flavor you could imagine."

"Do you have sour cream flavored?"

"I do. What size?"

"Small, please."

She places a small bag on the counter that seemed to be

between us. "Can I get you anything else?"

"No, thanks."

She looked me in the eye. "I must warn you, sir. Those will make you so thirsty you'd think you'd eaten a block of salt."

"So, I might want to buy a drink?"

She had a twinkle in her eye. "If you're not going to be near anything to drink, I recommend getting something."

"A small lemonade then too, please."

"I think you'll be happy with that," she said as she put a bottle of lemonade next to the bag of crisps. "Is there anything else I can entice you to buy?"

"No, thanks."

"You're all set then. Brilliant."

Angus stopped the action. "Fiona just demonstrated the second and the third C. Care to guess what they are?"

"Well, we connected but that's the first C. She asked me what I wanted, and she was courteous. How's that? Courtesy is the second C. I don't know what the third one would be."

Angus shook his head. "No. Courtesy is not the second C. It's more complicated than that."

"I thought you liked to keep things simple."

"I do," Angus laughed. "That I do. And you may have caught me. Early on, the 4 Cs were just one C: Caring. It seemed to me that if someone simply cared about doing a good job and cared about the needs of the customer, then all would be well. But we did many simulations and learned that it's a bit more complicated, but not much. Caring is one of the basics, along with energy and openness, but then we had to add some skill factors. It is a skill to connect human-to-human in just the right way. It's something that can be trained to a degree and that can be specific to the situation. You can connect more formally in a high-end restaurant and much more informally in a pub. But connect you must for good customer service. This gets us to Fiona and the second and third Cs. The second C is collaborating, that is, working with the customer to find out, from the customer's perspective, what is needed. You ken Fiona asking you all those questions about what you wanted?"

I nodded.

"The less you assume and the more you ask, the better the collaboration. The more you assume or the more you operate from a script or standards, the less you are able to collaborate. As much as you can be in the moment, be in the moment. You create the relationship with connecting human-to-human. You expand on that by collaborating. When done well, you know what the customer needs and the customer knows that you know. This is a very satisfactory situation. Do you understand collaborating?"

"Absolutely."

Angus continued without taking a breath. "The third C stands for Contributing. There are three parts to the third C and Fiona covered them quite well. To foster customer loyalty once you have a good if not great product, you must provide service, information and respect; S-I-R.

Fiona provided excellent service. What you wanted was put right in front of you. It was exactly what you wanted, and you got it when you wanted. You got it how you wanted too although I suppose she could have offered to open the crisps for you, warmed them up and put them on a plate, but that would have been overdoing it.

She provided information. You might have enjoyed the first few crisps, but very soon you would have wished for something to slack your thirst. She anticipated that and gave you information you didn't even know you needed. Information is probably what separates great service from just good service. Information comes in many forms. It could be as simple as suggesting to someone that they plan extra time getting to the store because of construction on the High Street or as esoteric as telling the customer about a 'work-around' that you found helpful with a new software program. "Why didn't you tell me that?' is a question you never want to hear from a customer. Did you notice how she gave you respect?"

"Yes, I did. She treated me as if my buying a bag of crisps was the most important transaction of the day. I could feel that. I think she called me 'sir' once and it fit into the flow of the conversation. It wasn't as if she was trying to work it in as a courtesy. And giving me the information about the saltiness of the crisps. That respected me too."

"Aye. You ken how respect is much like connecting. If it's artificial, it doesn't count. In fact, it detracts from what you're trying to create. These three elements, service, information, and respect overlap quite a bit. Part of great service is to be deferential to the needs of the customer. Providing them information is respecting their needs, too. All three are necessary in just the right amounts."

"Like not informing a woman who is shopping for a recliner for her husband all about leather chairs she has no interest in."

"Exactly right. Now think of the greatest customer service experience you ever had. Something that made you think that you would always return to that place."

I thought for a moment. What popped into my head was a recent experience I had at my bank. According to them, I had bounced two checks even though I had enough money in my account to cover them. The bank had made a mistake, but two companies I sent checks to, were not happy with me. "I went to my bank," I said, "to straighten out a mistake they made and talked with this account manager who was just fantastic."

"What did he or she do?"

"She stood up from her desk as I approached. I thought that was great. I told her what had happened and said I was sorry to dump such a problem on her. She replied that she was there to solve problems, was apologetic that a problem had occurred and that she would make sure it was sorted out. I like how she took responsibility and apologized too."

"Did you feel connected?"

"Sure did. I sat down and she started looking through my account on her computer. She told me what she was doing as she did it."

"Information."

"Yes. And respect too, I would guess. Yeah, that's right. Service, information, and respect. They were all there. Interesting. Everything got fixed. I felt great."

"Part of the importance of information is that you don't want your customers to be uncertain. The more significant the transaction, the more important information is. Remember our doctor and patient and the fatal cancer diagnosis? That patient needed a tremendous amount of information and received only the worst part. Actually, the patient needed connecting human-to-human most and information only slowly as he could comprehend it." Angus held up his finger for emphasis. "What makes that circumstance particularly interesting is the heightened need for service, information and respect." Angus turned to the console. "Let's look at a couple of versions of the situation. Here's version one again."

The screen shows the old man sitting in the exam room when the door opens and the doctor walks in.

Doctor: Looking at the chart rather than the patient. "Hello, Mr. Jones. How are you today?"

Patient: "Fine, doctor. How are you?"

Doctor: "Well, you're here for your test results and I'm afraid they came back positive."

Patient: "Positive. That's good, isn't it?"

Doctor: "No, it's not good. Positive means you have cancer, pretty bad cancer. In fact, you have the worst form and, I'm sorry to say, it's into your organs."

Patient: Looking shocked. "Oh, my."

Doctor: "Yes. In the next few months your organs will begin to shut down and we'll have a hard time treating you."

The doctor's pager goes off. He takes it out and looks at it. "I'm afraid I have to make a phone call. Why don't you make an appointment for next week and we'll discuss this then."

The action on the screen stops. "This is what I saw," I said, before Angus could start. "No connecting human-to-human. The doctor was looking at the chart when he came in and didn't respond when the patient asked, 'how are you?' No collaboration, either, from what I saw. There was some service because the doctor gave the diagnosis, which we assume is correct. But there was no service beyond that and a brief description of what would happen down the road. Information was also minimal, and I would say respect was pretty lacking too."

"Exactly. Here's version two." The screen shows the same doctor entering the room.

Doctor:	Looking at the patient. "Hello, Mr. Jones. How are you today?"
Patient:	"Fine, doctor. How are you?"
Doctor:	"I'm fine too. It's good to see you again. Well, you're here for your test results and I'm afraid they came back positive."
Patient:	"Positive. That's good, isn't it?"

Doctor: "No, it's not good. And I'm sorry it isn't better news. Positive means you have cancer."

Patient: Looking shocked. "Oh, my."

Doctor: "Yes. I'm sorry. What you have is a form of malignancy centered in the globus paladus and the medulla oblingota. Over time this will result in symptoms of presenile dementia."

Patient: "Oh."

Doctor: "Yes. We can be aggressive at first, but I think we'd be best to think about palliative care."

Patient: "Whatever you say, doctor."

The action on the screen stops. "So, what do you think about this?" Angus asks.

"I think they connected. It was like the doctor and patient may have known each other for a while, so connecting was good. Still didn't see much of what I would call collaboration. It was better service, and I think better respect. But the doctor didn't really give useful information. I had no idea what he was talking about. And I guess that means he really didn't give good service or ultimately respect the patient."

Angus nodded. "When things are complex, like in the

doctor's exam room, the provider and the customer must work together to figure things out. You must work within the patient's frame of reference. Many doctors operate only from a medical perspective and practically ignore the real life of the patient."

"I caught how you said 'doctors operate...'"

Ignoring my reference to his pun, Angus continued. "In our example, the doctor had to elicit the patient's needs as well as he could and maybe just be there, waiting for the patient to sort things out. In all probability, the patient was not going to hear any information the doctor might want to give. This was a great opportunity to collaborate with the patient, find out how he saw the situation; at least an inkling of it and then both could work on what the patient required most at that moment. The service the patient needed was support and caring. Any information he needed he probably would ask for as he became aware of questions. Can you imagine the intense need for collaborating at such a moment to make sure the service is done well?"

Angus turned back to the console and the screen showed the exam room as before, the patient waiting for the doctor. Then the door opens, and the doctor enters.

Doctor:	Looking at the patient. "Hello, Mr. Jones. How are you today?"
Patient:	"Fine, doctor. How are you?"
Doctor:	"I'm fine, too. It's good to see you again. Well, you're here for your test

	results and I'm afraid they did not come back the way we had hoped."
Patient:	Looks a bit uncertain. "What do you mean?"
Doctor:	"The results came back positive for cancer. That means you have signs of cancer in your brain."
Patient:	Looking shocked. "Oh, my."
Doctor:	"Yes. I'm sorry."
Patient:	"What does this mean? Am I going to die?"
Doctor:	"Mr. Jones, it's way too early to know how this is going to progress. But I know this is tough news to digest." Puts his hand on the patient's arm. "What I want to do this morning is to learn as well as I can what this means to you so I can know how best to help."
Patient:	"This is all such a shock."
Doctor:	"Yes."

On the screen, the patient remained silent and the doctor waited for what would happen next. Then the screen went dark.

Angus turned to me with a questioning look.

"That was totally different," I said. "The doctor seemed to be waiting for the patient to tell him what needed to be done. The doctor didn't get into all sorts of medical jargon. In fact, his compassion was amazing."

"Aye. The best medical service he could give at that moment was totally dependent on what the patient needed to comprehend his diagnosis. Collaboration and contributing at their best."

"I remember when my wife was dying. I felt so helpless to do anything for her. I'd say her doctors were pretty good. I can see that some were more comfortable talking about the disease than talking to the patient."

Angus' face turned pale. "George, I should have switched to another example. I'm sorry."

"That's okay. I've been struggling with her death and what I was doing as she was going through it. I was so helpless. But we connected. We connected as well as two people could. That's a comfort. Now I'm asking myself: Did I contribute? I think I did. Everything she needed, I got. I tried to anticipate her needs, so she never wanted anything. I listened. I told her I loved her a million times."

"Every human interaction deserves no less. None of us has more than a finite number of moments on earth. How do we make them meaningful? We connect with each other. We collaborate to ensure defining mutual goals. We contribute to the betterment of mankind." Angus smiled. "I get carried away. Are you ready to talk about the fourth C?"

Notes

Collaborate so you and the customer are a unified team heading toward the same goal.

Contribute whatever your customer needs you to contribute.

Assuming your product is good, what your customer needs you to contribute is a combination of:
- Service
- Information
- Respect

Sometimes collaborating is the best way of contributing.

7

The Fourth C

It was nearing lunchtime. Angus suggested we return to the sitting room to talk about the fourth C and to discuss what we should do for lunch. I told him a pub lunch would be terrific and that I would buy. "Ah, you've warmed my Scottish soul with that offer," he said.

We had no sooner relaxed into the leather seats when Angus asked me what kind of car I drove. I told him a Cadillac. I enjoyed the luxury, it looked beautiful and it was the most reliable car I had ever owned. He then asked how much I knew about assembly lines.

I knew firsthand about assembly lines. Summers during college I worked on a General Motors line building quarter-ton trucks. I remembered the constant flow of panels that I spot-welded together, something like five hundred in a ten-hour shift. I learned the sequence of welds I was supposed to make in about ten minutes, and then repeated the same task until I did it in my sleep. Now, the same job is done by robots.

"If you made a mistake, what would happen?" he asked.

"If it was a small mistake, nothing. No one would notice. Maybe something would rattle on the truck after five years or fifty thousand miles, I don't know. If it was a big mistake, I was supposed to stop the line so it could get fixed."

"Were there inspectors?"

"Oh, yeah. You know this. With the assembly process, everything was standardized, and tolerances were known. You could check every fiftieth car and have a good idea how things were going, yet each car had things inspected. But in those days, the customer was the final inspector, and a few got lemons. Car dealers were comfortable fixing a few things here and there to keep the customer satisfied and it helped the customer bond better with after-sale service. Up to a point, anyway. If too much had to be fixed, it often ended in a war between customer, dealer, and factory. Where are you headed?"

"Value stream. Each step in the assembly process is supposed to be adding value to the product for the customer. Since we're not perfect, some steps don't add value. Some even reduce value. When you buy your Cadillac, you expect it to be in great shape. You don't care much about the value stream. You care about the end product, right?"

"Yes, but I care about the value stream being efficient. Otherwise, I'm paying too much for the car."

"Correct, but the important moment of truth is when you turn the key and drive off in your new car."

"Right."

"The idea is that for many customers much of the value stream is invisible. This means that quality control can be intermittent as long as the end product is the best it can be. And, as you mentioned, so long as rework and other inefficiencies don't affect the final quality-price ratio. All this gets interesting with the customer service value stream.

Unlike attaching doors to a car body, where you can rework it later if necessary and the customer is not affected, customer service value streams directly impact the customer every step of the way. The best assembly processes mistake-proof as well as possible and each worker is an inspector, and for the most part, standardization is the backbone for quality.

This works many places in service too, like fast food where consistency is more valued than personal service. Service quality is kept within the bounds expected by the customer. But in my mind, the concept of standardization has been overused and reduces customer satisfaction. Managers believe that service quality control can be done the same way as an assembly process, so they train employees to handle customers in a standard way, like an assembly process.

Many places sample customer satisfaction with yearly surveys. Others have comment cards available for those inclined to fill them out. Still others employ mystery shoppers or use other methods to measure customer service.

We talked just a while ago about all a customer's moments of truth adding together to make a value stream. That value stream can start with advertising and end with the billing process. Unlike an assembly process that can be sampled for quality, the customer service value stream must have each moment of truth monitored for quality every time."

"I'm getting the feeling that checking is the fourth C."

"Very close. The fourth C is confirm, not just check. As much as humanly possible, every moment of truth needs to be confirmed as meeting the customer's needs and expectations and hopes. That can't be done of course, and if it was, it might drive the customer loony.

Our computer-generated mother at the birthday party thought that as soon as things calmed down a bit, she would make sure the gift she got for her son was exactly the right one. She might ask once, maybe twice if she was unsure, but more than that would make the lad irritated. We have the task of figuring out how much confirming is useful and how to do that."

"Angus, remember the snack guy on the train? You said he missed every part of good customer service. He didn't say anything but 'Ta' after we paid. No confirmation at all. And none of the other Cs either."

"Because he didn't care, had no energy and was as closed to the here and now as a dead man. In that situation, to confirm he could have repeated what our orders were as he handed them to us and ask if we would like anything else."

"Confirming seems simple enough," I said, foolishly.

"On the contrary. You must be astute enough to confirm in such a way that any service problems are brought to light. That's why you confirm. It is not to seal the deal so much as it is to make the most of a last chance to make everything perfect. I've had many an experience in American diners where you go to a cashier to pay the bill. The person behind the register will take your money and without looking at you ask if everything was all right. If everything wasn't all right, would you say anything? Usually not. The confirming, actually in this case the checking, was too late and too little."

"I have to agree. Most of the time if service or whatever isn't quite right, I don't say anything, but if the person asking seems genuinely interested, then I'm more likely to tell them. Like at a restaurant if my baked potato isn't quite done and the server asks, 'Is everything all right?' I usually just say 'yes.'"

"That's because you didn't have clear instructions that it was better to say 'no.' If your baked potato is warm enough, you don't want to disrupt your and everyone else's dinner to wait for a hotter one to arrive some time later.

George, picture yourself out for dinner and your potato is not cooked through. It's not hot and is somewhat hard in the middle, but not so bad that you would normally say anything. The server comes by and says, 'I hope everything is satisfactory. Sir, how is your potato? Sometimes they don't get cooked all the way through.' What would you say?"

"I'd say my potato wasn't cooked enough."

"And why would you do that?"

I smiled. "Because the server told me I should."

Angus smiled, too. "Can you imagine an organization that knows its strengths and weaknesses so well that it can ask the customer specifically if something is not up to snuff? Your server knew that sometimes potatoes can be baked the right amount of time and be hot to the touch, but not be fully cooked. By asking specifically about the potato, two things occurred. You had a specific quality question directed at you that you were encouraged to answer and also probably felt encouraged to bring up any other problem that had occurred. There was no half-hearted 'is everything all right?'"

"So, you try to confirm in an encouraging way at each moment of truth of the value stream without driving the customer crazy?"

"In a word, 'yes.' But you don't have to just confirm. You can confirm, collaborate, contribute and connect human-to-human all at the same time."

"I'd like to see how that would work."

Angus immediately got up from his chair, came over to me and shook my hand. "I'm so pleased to meet you Mr. Corbett. With all the road construction I hope you were able to find your way into the parking lot okay." Angus let go of my hand. "And you would say that you managed it all right and I would say, 'When we're finished here, I'll show you an easier way to get back to the main road.' We've begun to connect. I've done an initial bit of confirming of your experience so far and I'm going to collaborate with you so I can contribute to your return trip." Angus sat back in his chair.

"That's pretty good. I can see that you get connected early and do your best to stay connected..."

"Let me interrupt. There is a very good way of ensuring being connected as long as possible and it is so simple it makes me cringe whenever it is missed. When the business has been transacted and the customer is leaving, often they will say, 'thank you,' exactly what we want. Then we lose a wonderful opportunity. So many employees will respond with a cheery, 'no problem' or 'uh huh' or something equally ill-suited to customer service.

When the customer has the grace to say, 'thank you,' look that customer in the eye and say clearly and distinctly, 'You're welcome' and mean every wonderful syllable of that phrase. That keeps you connected 'till the very last."

"I like that. That certainly ties together the concept and the behavior. But I need to get a better handle on how you confirm along the entire value stream. You said it should be done, that it can't be done, and if it could be done it would drive the customer crazy. I have to assume that you end up doing like the car-makers, sampling every so often."

"Alas you do, but in such a way every moment of truth has a good chance to be evaluated and certainly the customer ends up feeling special. Let's look at a patient going to the doctor's office. The patient might see four different people, the receptionist, the nurse, the doctor and the billing clerk. Each one of those people can confirm his or her portion of the value stream and in general, the elements of the value stream that came before.

The first person, the receptionist, can ask about parking and, of course, anything that he or she does. The next person, the nurse, can ask about the wait in the waiting room and so on. At the end, the patient might even be asked to rate the entire experience on a board in the waiting room for all to see. What a reward for the staff and an encouragement for the patients to see a host of 'Excellents' on the board. We can talk more about that later. But you get the idea, right?"

"Yes. Confirm satisfaction in a way that maximizes being told whatever the person isn't satisfied with and do that for each moment of truth along the value stream in a way that makes the customer feel special and doesn't drive them crazy. Got it."

"How about lunch at the Horse and Hound?"

Notes

Each step of the customer service value stream should unequivocally add value to the customer's experience.

The customer service value stream does best when there is customer input with every moment of truth.

Confirm satisfaction in a way that encourages the expression of dissatisfaction.

Stay Connected Human-to-Human as long as possible.

8

The Search for Accountability

If you're in the right mood, Scottish pubs are glorious places. Inside the Horse and Hound was a bar near the far wall, benches along the other three walls and half a dozen tables in the middle. We were lucky. All the tables but one were occupied. We walked through the door and headed toward the empty table.

"Ho, Duncan," Angus hailed the barman, raising his arm and waving.

"Afternoon, Professor," the barman answered.

As we passed one of the tables, the three men sitting there said in unison, "Afternoon, Doctor." Angus responded, "Hey, lads."

As we sat at our table, I looked at Angus. "Professor and Doctor. I don't know much about you, do I?"

"They like to say those things. I think they like the fact

that an academic comes into their neighborhood pub. The professor bit comes from my appointment at the University of St. Andrews across the Tay. They have a wonderful international relations program and I am proud to be a part of it. I teach there twice a week. That's where I got my Ph.D. and I was lucky enough that they wanted to keep me."

"You have a doctorate. That's not on your card, but that's why the 'doctor' too?"

"Actually, no. I attended medical school first. But the M.D. isn't relevant for what I do now."

I'm sure my raised eyebrows prompted him to quickly tell me more.

"Over here, you don't have to go to undergraduate school before medical school. I started at seventeen and finished quite early. I didn't practice after training. My intention was to go into psychiatry. I wanted to understand what makes people tick. I soon realized I wasn't so much interested in what went on inside someone as what they did with each other. That led to attending St. Andrews. My research interests led me into this project, and I have been learning a tremendous amount ever since. I started out seeking to better understand cultural differences. If anything could have been, that was my specialty. In fact, when it comes to customer service, if I wrote a book on the subject, I'd have to add that cultural differences play a part, but if you do the 4 Cs well enough, not too large a part."

"So, customer service is just a small part of what you're doing."

"Understanding human interactions is what I do, all types. Customer service is as good an interaction to study as any and it does allow testing of a lot of models. Ah, here's Duncan."

The portly barman stood at our table. "Gentlemen," he said looking at each of us in turn. "I hope it's lunch you'll be wanting. The lasagna is the best we've ever had. That and a glass of our best red would make a meal fit for royalty."

Angus looked at me, then turned to Duncan. "If my friend agrees, make that two lasagnas and two glasses of red."

"Sounds good to me," I said.

"Won't be but a minute. I'll fetch your silver and bring you the wine." Duncan turned and walked toward what I guessed was the kitchen.

Within ten minutes, Angus and I were digging into a lasagna still steaming from the oven with a side of mushy peas and drinking a robust red wine of indeterminate origin. "This is terrific," I said, in spite of my mouth being full. I looked at the rest of the crowd. "A popular place."

"Aye. There is a lesson in that."

"Why doesn't that surprise me? Are you on duty all the time?"

"I love observing and learning. Everywhere you go people are interacting. Looking and listening can teach you far more than any theory or model. You're right. This place is very popular. On Fridays and Saturdays, there is a queue outside until near closing time. That's rare for a place as removed as this."

"I'll bite. How come?"

Angus smiled. "Another truth about customer service and creating loyal customers. Like Fiona, Duncan owns the establishment. He is solely responsible for its success or failure. You can be sure he does everything he can to ensure repeat customers. If you're to have any chance of confirming satisfaction along the service value stream, someone has to be accountable to do that. At the Horse and Hound, that is relatively easy. Duncan works many hours and strictly oversees what little extra help he hires. In any system, someone has to be the last one accountable. Make everyone accountable and no one is accountable. Even with the best model and the 4 Cs is the best so far, customer service is an elusive behavior, and someone has to be the captain to ensure reliability."

Angus opens his arms to draw my attention to the full room. "What do you see when you look at all these people and all this activity?"

"A thriving business?"

"Aye. But, look some more. Remember what we briefly talked about before coming out to lunch? I mentioned the doctor's waiting room with a board filled with 'excellents.' It was the idea of a public display of customer satisfaction. Remember?"

"Yes."

"Watch Duncan."

I watched Duncan. When time permitted, he went from table to table, asking how things were. He asked specifics. How was the stout? How was the fish? And he thanked each one for coming in. At one table a man held up his plate of lasagna. "Peas are cold, Duncan," he said. Duncan took the plate and quickly returned with a new one, with double the original amount of peas, this time they were steaming like the lasagna.

Angus poked me with his elbow. "Can you imagine a more public display of a high level of service as that? Asking each table, more than once, and very specifically how things are. You can tell Duncan really wants to know so he can fix any problems immediately. I'll bet your salespeople at Superior Furniture can't solve customer complaints right away."

"Furniture sales is a bit more complicated than heating up a plate of peas," I said, somewhat defensively.

"Agreed, but we're not talking complicated. We're talking accountability. The idea is for everyone to be as accountable as Duncan is. The problem is most people see a complaint as a problem."

"It is. Something went wrong and somebody is unhappy. Not many people enjoy dealing with someone who is complaining to them."

Angus held up that finger of his again. "Complaints are a problem if you don't have a good way of handling them. Take Duncan for example. He probably hears ten, maybe twenty complaints a day. You know why?" Angus kept going. "He asks to hear problems, that's why. People have learned to look forward to presenting Duncan a problem because they know it will be a positive experience. You have a store in America, Nordstrom. That company is famous, even over here, for how well it handles customer complaints. Their employees have a simple concept, don't let a customer leave the store unhappy. They know that identifying problems is a good way to uncover things that should be improved. Hospitals are becoming the same way. They want to discover treatment errors as quickly as possible. Many organizations are creating safety alert processes to highlight errors so fewer will be made. If we can make service, and in the case of hospitals, safety, a transparent process, we can perfect it.

Workers on assembly lines are often given bonuses for finding and fixing problems, we should do the same with any employee who discovers a customer service error. Rewarding accountability, my good man, is critical. Few organizations know how to do it well."

I pointed both my index fingers at Angus. "And you have an idea."

"You may have noticed, George, that I like metaphors. The birthday party is one. An assembly line is another. Think of all the maintenance an assembly line receives. The system is regularly oiled, parts are replaced, things are fixed as soon as they break. We should do the same for the customer service value stream. We don't though. We assume things are fine and don't pay nearly as much attention to human interactions as they deserve. Think of an assembler bolting two pieces together and compare that to an employee talking with a customer. Which action is more fraught with danger and which action is more examined? A simple bolt tightening is analyzed to the nth degree. When it comes to understanding human interactions, the knee-jerk reaction is to try to increase control of the verbal interchange. That's when scripts and standards are born. A better response it to make this action more transparent and the employee more accountable for its outcome."

"But how do you make someone accountable for something you don't want standardized? It's unfair to tell employees to be themselves, then punish them when it doesn't work out."

"When what doesn't work out?"

"The transaction. The sale. Customer service. Customer satisfaction. All of it."

"How do you measure customer service success at Superior Furniture?"

I was beginning to hate this part. I had to clarify what we did, and Angus always found what we did to be wrong. He always had a better way. Twenty-four hours ago, I would have been proud to explain what my company did for customer service. Now it seemed like we were in the dark ages. But I was learning. I knew that each problem that we uncovered meant a better solution. So, I answered. "We judge on sales volume, both number of sales and dollar amounts, Store volume, footage and traffic, any complaints or compliments and quarterly evaluations."

"Does your sales staff talk amongst themselves?"

"I suppose so."

"But you don't measure that."

"No."

"Does your sales staff talk to the clerical staff?"

"Probably, but not much I wouldn't think."

"Hmm."

"What, hmm?"

"Knowing what you know now about the 4 Cs and if you wanted to change what you measure, what would you measure?"

I thought for a moment. Then another penny dropped. "I'd measure the 4 Cs."

"You'd measure how well they connected human-to-human, how well they collaborated and contributed, and how well they confirmed?"

"Yes. And before you ask, I don't know how I would do that off-hand."

Angus frowned. "George, how long can you stay today?"

"Oh, I know, Angus. I've taken up far more of your time

than I should." I reached into my pocket for the train schedule.

Angus patted my arm. "That is not what I meant. We're sliding into how to create loyal staff and I wanted to make sure you had the time to discuss this topic. I have all the long day. This is what I do and I'm very much enjoying myself."

"I have as much time as you have."

"Good. Duncan and Fiona are good examples of how measuring customer satisfaction should be done. They are also good examples of how to ensure your staff are loyal, too."

I motioned to Gordon for two more glasses of wine. Angus was winding himself up again.

"I'm biased toward the significance of relationships. That's one reason why I think all businesses are ninety-five percent service. This bias led me to look at relationships and in what we're talking about today, how they relate to promoting customer and employee loyalty. That, naturally enough, led me to look at how to measure. You see, measuring customer satisfaction by what customers say, like in surveys and the like, misses half the equation, your employees. I think you measure customer satisfaction and by good fortune staff satisfaction, by looking at the relationship between customer and employee. It is in that relationship where the magic lies."

"I never would have thought about that."

"But it makes sense doesn't it?"

As I was thinking, Duncan brought over two glasses of wine and cleared away our now empty lasagna plates. "Any interest in desert, gentlemen?" he asked.

Angus looked at me and I shook my head. "No, thank you, Duncan," Angus told him, "but as always, the lasagna was superb."

"Thank you. The seasoning. Was it to your liking?" Duncan looked at each of us for confirmation.

"Couldn't have been better," I said. "Thank you."

Duncan bowed his head. "You're very welcome. It was my pleasure." He smiled and returned to the bar.

"Sometimes," Angus said, rubbing his forehead, "I think all I have to do to understand great customer service is to buy lunch here and a double nugget wafer at Fiona's. I could put together a model of what they do, publish the results and I'd be famous. Instead, I have to create a million models and test them to death. But what do you think, my friend? Is the relationship between customer and employee the critical point in service?"

"Well, Angus, I guess that the customer-employee relationship; their interaction, is where the action is. Where else could it be? But I still don't know how you would measure that."

"In the lab, I measure it by the emotional reaction of the customer and employee. I can do that for every type of relationship, every type of interaction you could name. In the real world, you can't do that. That's why we're on the border between customer and employee satisfaction. You see, if you do it right, the only way to do it right in fact, the customer's satisfaction is dependent on the employee and the employee's satisfaction is dependent on the customer.

There is considerable research supporting the idea that higher staff satisfaction leads to better customer satisfaction. The way I figure it, the key measure should be the relationship between employee and customer. The better that is, the better everyone is. You've seen what happens with some married couples. One's happy, the other isn't. Both have to be happy to make it work. Same is true in business. In fact, a recent Gallup poll in America, assessing a million and a half workers, found that over seventy-two percent of employees were emotionally disconnected from their work. Do you think many of that group provide good customer service to their customers? Not on your life. And remember, the definition of customer includes co-workers: peers, managers, subordinates, everyone. The state of the worker is unnecessarily horrible and can be fixed. I'll tell you what. Why don't we finish up here, make our way back to the lab, and I'll show you what I mean?"

Notes

Every organization should have one person accountable for the quality of service and that person should be a senior executive.

Make service as transparent and public a process as possible.

Make each employee clearly responsible to Connect Human-to-Human, to Collaborate, to Contribute, and to Confirm.

The relationship between customer and employee is the critical point in service.

9

If the Formula Fits

We were back in the lab. Angus had given me the parameters for the computer simulation, and I was saying them to the computer. "Group of three furniture employees hired for caring, openness and energy, great at every "C," connecting human-to-human, collaborating, contributing and confirming. They are discussing the day's work."

The screen displayed two women and a man having coffee while sitting at a round table. Angus added, "Their names are Teresa, Deanne, and Harry."

"Hold it, Angus. I want to go back to just customer service for a moment. Is that okay?" We needed to review some topics I thought had been overlooked. I'm not a cynic, but I am a realist. Angus had me convinced that his 4 Cs was a powerful approach, but he had neglected two important areas of customer service. I wondered how his model would handle them. When he said go ahead, I did.

"What about dissatisfied customers? We have a very useful approach we learned from Development Dimensions International."

"Aye, taking the H.E.A.T. I know it well. There are many others. One I heard about the other day is L.A.F.F.: Listen, Apologize, Form a plan, Follow the plan. Is that the sort of thing you mean?"

"Yes. In a way, using that acronym combines standards and scripts, and they're easily remembered and easily applied."

"They work very well. And you're wondering if they are better at handling problems than what I've been suggesting?"

"Yes. Actually, I'm wondering if you avoided talking about dissatisfied customers because your approach didn't cope with them very well."

"Fair enough. Would you prefer an explanation or a demonstration?"

"Just your thoughts would be fine."

"Approaches like taking the H.E.A.T. and L.A.F.F. and the rest of them work very well because they give the person under fire from an angry customer a tool to use when the going is tough. Trying to think of the right thing to say when you're being attacked is not easy. They are also good because you can practice using them in a safe training environment. They also work well because they follow good interactive guidelines. Do you want to know the technique that has worked best in the lab?"

"Sure. But let me guess, the 4 Cs."

"Of course. And I'll show you why. You are the dissatisfied customer. I'm the employee." Angus leaned toward me and shook my hand. "Hello, Mr. Corbett, I'm Angus McTavish. I understand there is a problem and I'm going to do everything necessary to resolve it." He leaned away from me. "What do you think of that for a start?"

"Pretty strong. You were connecting with me and giving me information and I guess providing me the beginning of a service and showing me respect. Impressive."

"And all in the same model we've been talking about. But what if you were extremely angry and your response to me was something like, 'I don't care if you're the Queen of England, I want a new recliner and I want it now.' Now that would be tough, wouldn't it?"

I nodded, remembering some of my floor experiences that didn't go well.

"If the person is so angry that we don't connect human to human, you don't force that, but let it evolve while you focus on gathering and exchanging information. Let me show you why." Angus stands up and walks over to a white board along the wall to the right of the screen. He picks up a blue marker and writes:

$$F = E - R$$

"You like formulas, George. I'll wager you haven't seen this one. What this means is that frustration is equal to the gap between what someone expects and what reality is. Let's say our irate shopper bought a recliner from your store ten years earlier. His mechanism has recently broken, and he wants you to give him a brand-new chair for nothing."

"That's absurd, but I've heard worse."

"Aye. Now you have a choice to make. Do you want to retain this person as a customer? Would pushing him out of the store result in him complaining to others about his ill-treatment in your store? Would people who know him believe him and repeat his story causing a ripple of discontent within their circle? Do you want to salvage what you can? Do your best for this complainer? Understanding this formula will help you decide what to do and how to respond."

"I'm listening. As you said, I like formulas."

"You use the formula to determine what the person expected and what the reality is. In our example, the man expected his chair would last forever and he expected that your store would provide him a new one since his chair was obviously, to him anyway, defective. The reality is different. Chairs wear out. Your store doesn't give away furniture. So we have a huge gap between expectations and reality. In this case, your customer has an erroneous expectation, so that is where we begin. You be the customer and I'll follow the 4 Cs to see if we can make this right. Collaboration in this case is for me to understand your expectations and for you to know what the reality is, and then I'll try to make reality and expectations equal one another."

"Okay," I said. Then, as angry as I could make it, "My chair fell apart this morning and I almost broke my arm. What are you going to do about it? I want a new chair."

"Yes, sir. I'm glad to help out. And I apologize for what happened. May I ask you for a few details?"

"Why, so you can weasel out of your responsibility?"

Angus laughs. "No, sir. I want to find out how I can best help you."

"This isn't a laughing matter," I said, as sternly as I could muster.

"No, sir. My responsibility is to be on your side, and I don't want to weasel out of that. I assume you bought the chair here. How long ago was that?"

"Ah, maybe ten years or so. But that doesn't mean it should just fall apart."

"No, sir, it doesn't. We pride ourselves in selling quality furniture. Now when you said it fell apart, exactly what happened?"

"The foot rest fell off, and the whole thing wobbled."

"Mr. Corbett, I think I know what happened. Over time, bolts can work loose in recliners and sometimes they come all the way out. Have you noticed bolts lying near your chair lately?"

"Hmm. Yeah, I guess I have. Didn't know what they could be."

Angus formed his hands into a "T" calling for a time out. "Here you have choice depending on what you want to do. Did you sense an improving human-to-human connection as we went along? As I was gathering information, you were calming down and I hope feeling respected due to my sincere apology and that I was giving you good customer service. Did you feel that?"

"Yes, that was pretty apparent."

"So, if I wanted to keep you as a satisfied customer, I could make an offer to you that one of our technicians go out to your house and tighten the bolts or whatever else needed to be done, free of charge. Then I would confirm to make sure that doing that was the best solution for you. If, on the other hand, you didn't calm down and we didn't begin to connect human-to-human, I would know that no matter what the reality, I was not going to meet your expectations. Once I recognized this, I would try to offer amends that would get you out of the store as quickly and easily as possible. This is where working with the public can get scary. My rule of thumb is that if you cannot even begin to connect, the situation could turn ugly, so it needs to be handled immediately. Predetermined amends work as well as anything in this situation.

The script type techniques you mentioned are useful ways of connecting. Listening, apologizing, working together to find a plan, all steps with the outcome of connecting and contributing. To understand the customer's frustration, you need to exchange information to find the difference between expectation and reality."

"Some customers are more than just frustrated," I reminded him.

Angus, who was still standing by the white board, turned to write on it again. Under the first formula he wrote:

$$A = F + h$$

"This formula says that anger is a combination of frustration and hurt. But the degree of frustration is much greater than the hurt. Here's another formula."

$$D = f + H$$

"This one says that depression is a combination of frustration and hurt with hurt being primary. Now psychologists and other social scientists would say that anger and depression are much more complicated than what I have shown, but I just want to make a point about improving customer service. The idea is that the angry customer has been frustrated, that is, either the customer's expectations have not been met or that the reality experienced was not satisfactory, and this is intense enough or has gone on long enough to evolve into anger. Let's say you sold a defective chair. The expectation of a good chair was reasonable, and the reality was not. So you would address the reality and fix the problem. With an angry customer, you know either E or R is bad and additionally, that the person has some emotional hurt to deal with. What better way to handle hurt than connecting human-to-human?"

"With irate customers, you don't do anything different?"

"No, just use some of that energy, caring and openness we hired you for and do the 4 Cs as well as they can be done."

"I have another area that I'm wondering about."

"Have at it."

"The telephone. If I were to set up an automated telephone system, how could I make it the most customer friendly it can be and still hold down costs? I don't want to hire expert furniture people to handle all my phone calls, but I sure like the idea of connecting human-to-human."

Angus returned to the chair and sat next to me.

"Interesting question and we looked at that, too. The telephone is often the first contact between business and customer, we don't want to do that poorly. You know I would say you want to connect human-to-human first, as well as you can, as quickly as you can and that means the phone is answered by a live person. I suppose your question is, can you have an auto-attendant phone system and still provide great service. Can you have one of those dastardly phone trees of pushing one then six then four and never getting what you need?"

I shrugged. "Yeah, I suppose that's what I was wondering."

"The answer, George, may surprise you. Yes, you can."

"That does surprise me. How can you connect human-to-human with a robot voice and a phone tree?"

"Although great service requires you to connect, you don't have to connect every time. If I bought a couch at your store and I expected delivery in three weeks and you had a website where I could track the delivery process, would I need to connect with anyone? No. Same with an auto-attendant. If I make a call for simple information and can get it quickly through a phone system, that's the service and information I need in the best way. However, if I'm uncertain about something, say I have a fever and am worried that my old malaria problem is recurring, I want to talk to a person, not a recording.

An auto-attendant has a lot of advantages; it will always show up for work on time, is perfectly consistent, is never moody, can respond quickly to common questions and so on, but," Angus shook his head, "it can't be human. It can't answer unusual questions, it can't calm someone down, and it can't create a new problem-solving approach when that is the right thing to do."

"Then the auto-attendant is great service for quick and simple information. But we must determine what part of our phone system can best handle which of the 4 Cs. That takes us back to who your customers are, what they need, and how to meet their need."

"That's what you and I have been doing, you know."

"What?"

"We've been connecting human-to-human. I've been contributing; a service, information, and respect. What do you think about that?"

"It's exactly the right thing to do."

"We've been good partners. If you've a mind to, I think it's time to discuss how everything we have looked at so far about paying customers also applies to all those other people who make up a business. It all relates to how the 4 Cs are applied to teamwork." Angus motioned to the screen where the two women and the man were sitting at a table having coffee. "We have Teresa, Deanne, and Harry waiting for us."

Notes

Customer service tools such as scripts and mnemonics are useful sometimes in stressful situations especially when the customer has no intention of creating a Human-to-Human connection.

Usually, trying to Connect Human-to-Human is the best first step in changing an unhappy customer into a happy one.

If you cannot establish a Human-to-Human connection with a customer, you may be better off not having that person as a customer.

10

End the Workday Happy

Angus reset the scene for me. He said in some future time, after I returned to Orlando and implemented a few ideas, this is what would happen at one of Superior Furniture's stores. The three employees were relaxing in a comfortable staff lounge.

Teresa: Putting down her cup of coffee. "So, Deanne, how was your day?"

Deanne: "Great. Couldn't have been better. I had eight customers, seven of them said 'thank you' about as strongly as it can be said and the eighth one looked me in the eye and said, 'I can't believe

Teresa:	"That's great. Your goal is 90% 'thank yous and you got 100% today. You're right can't get better than that. Well done. Harry, how about you?"
Harry:	"Not so good, I'm afraid. I had ten customers. Five went well, two so-so and three I just couldn't connect with. That was discouraging."
Teresa:	"What do you think was going on?"
Harry:	Shakes his head. "I don't know. Maybe I was trying too hard."
Deanne:	"Harry asked me to observe his customer service after the first bad one. We thought maybe he was pushing too much so he eased off with the rest of them. The second one he didn't connect with was a young guy looking for a cheap TV stand. He was in and out so quick, I don't know who could have connected with him. I don't think it was anything about Harry."
Teresa:	"What about the other ones, the two so-so and the other unconnected one?"

the service you people provide.'"

Harry: "The unconnected one was my fault, I think. He looked like he had money and was looking at all sorts of top-of-the-line furniture. I thought he might buy out the store. I think I pushed to be his best friend ever."

Teresa: "So next time...?"

Harry: "I'll let things unfold. As for the so-so duo, the same thing. Maybe I had too much caffeine. I don't think I connected because I was pushing rather than relating. I learned my lesson, I think."

Deanne: "Harry, want me to observe a couple of interactions tomorrow?"

Harry: "Yeah, that'd help."

Teresa: "You guys work so well as a team. How were sales?"

Harry: "I did well there."

Deanne: "Me, too."

Teresa: "Anything I can do for you? Harry, could I help?"

Harry: "We'll see after tomorrow."

Deanne: "I'm fine."

Teresa: Getting up from the table. "Thanks, Deanne. Thanks, Harry. It is a pleasure to work with you. See you tomorrow."

Angus stopped the action. Although this was an interesting vignette, I had no idea what it was about. So, I asked. "Angus, what was that all about?"

He laughed. "I didn't tell you. You went back and hired a vice president of happiness for Superior Furniture."

"A vice president of happiness?"

"Yes. It's Teresa's job to debrief every employee every day to make sure they're happy. Great job, isn't it?"

"Sounds impossible."

"It is for one person to make each of your employees happy, but I wanted to make a point. Every researcher accepts that you can't have loyal customers if you have unhappy staff. Even if you have happy staff, you aren't guaranteed loyal customers. Your happy staff can be playing video games all day and treat customers as a distraction. What you want is your customers to say, 'I'm so happy I shopped at Superior Furniture today.' You want your staff to say essentially the same thing at the end of the workday, 'I'm really glad I work at Superior Furniture.'" You want loyal employees.

"So that's the ultimate target."

"Aye."

"I sure would like to achieve that."

"It won't be easy."

"No. I would imagine there is a lot of work to get staff to do the 4 Cs."

Angus shook his head. "That's not where the problem lies. The effort is in getting management to change. You'll need a completely different mindset if you want to have a good chance of reaching your goal. You'll have to allow your staff to be much less professional."

Oh, boy. So far, most of what Angus has suggested made good sense. It wasn't so touchy-feely that it would be a tough sell back home. But professionalism was a different matter. We prided ourselves on taking inexperienced and even experienced people and making them into highly competent professionals. This was true at every level and in every area of the organization. If you weren't professional, how could you be doing the best job? I gave Angus the sharpest look of skepticism I could muster.

"You're wondering if I'm daft."

"That's exactly what I'm wondering."

"Have no fear. This will make sense. How do you define professionalism?" Angus, of course, didn't give me time to answer. "It's when the job is more important than the person. It's when the worker stays after quitting time to get the job done. It's when the salesclerk absorbs the unfair anger of a customer to ensure a sale. Any time a worker puts self-interest after company interest, that's a professional attitude. Would you agree?"

"I would agree to that. In fact, that's a very good definition."

"So, if we want our employees to be professional, what

happens to all the connecting human-to-human we've been talking about?"

I sensed we were about to go down an Angus McTavish road to reach an Angus McTavish foregone conclusion. "I suppose you can do both. It doesn't have to be either/or," I replied.

"Ah, George, it does have to be either/or. You have to connect human-to-human with the customer first and the company has to connect human-to-human with its employees first. If the company meets its employees' needs first, then the employees will do their all to make the company a success. It cannot be the other way around. It cannot be done at the same time. The employee must initiate the connection with the customer and the company has to initiate the connection with the employee. And, it must be in an emotional way. If you picture connecting human-to-human as two people shaking hands, the rules of professionalism would have them saluting one another from exactly six feet apart. Doesn't work."

"You can't mean that being professional is a bad thing in business."

"I told you this would be difficult."

"It doesn't make sense."

"Business should be serious. It's like a war out there, isn't it?"

"Yes, it is. No one is going to give you success on a silver platter. War is exactly what it is. If you lose, your business dies."

Angus smiled. Something was coming. "You know, present day business is set up like military campaigns have been conducted for thousands of years. The general decides the strategy and leads the troops into battle and relies on senior and junior officers to communicate orders and for the foot soldiers to carry them out. Every officer and man would do or die for the cause. Sometimes it comes down to hand-to-hand combat, one man battling another man."

Angus paused for a moment, as if waiting for me to comment, but I held my tongue. "But you know, in business, we don't want our foot soldiers to kill anyone. We want them to connect, not simply do whatever leadership told them to do. Soldiers must follow lawful orders no matter what. But what's right in business is what's right for the customer in the moment. Maybe it doesn't work to wait for orders from above. Even modern armies rely more on quick thinking in the field to enable them to overcome standard orders that don't fit the current picture.

Maybe top down doesn't work so well in business anymore either. Maybe our foot soldiers should have more autonomy to react one to one in a positive way with customers. Maybe professionalism isn't what it used to be. Maybe our foot soldiers should have more fun. If I sent you a memo about an important contract and include a joke right in the middle, would that be unprofessional?"

"Yes."

"What would it harm?"

"I suppose it really wouldn't harm anything, but it would be silly. A distraction, a waste of valuable time."

"Would it be a way of connecting?"

"I suppose so."

"Do you think being professional is taking things seriously?"

"Absolutely, and I'm not talking military serious if you're looking to go that route again."

"Is being serious the goal of being professional?"

Yep, we were traveling the Angus highway to Angus land. "You can be serious and still connect. Being sincere is one way of connecting and that is very serious."

"Right you are. I may be exaggerating, but I'm also suggesting the connecting is either/or and that the company has to be first in connecting with employees and the employee has to be first in connecting with customers. This goes back to some of Aristotle's ideas. If you want to truly connect, you have to eliminate ulterior motives. You have to truly connect with the other person, and if that holds, you're set to do business, serious business.

Let's take a slightly different look at this. I mentioned Len Berry's book earlier, *The Soul of Service*. Soul. Does that sound professional? Not in the least. Then, there's Lencioni's thinking on teams. He talks about the..."

"I know where you're headed. Lack of trust is the basic flaw in dysfunctional teams. Trust certainly has to be part of connecting. But trust also is part of being professional. The customer can trust that you'll do the right thing."

"Do you trust a friend more than you do a stranger? Do you trust someone you care about more than someone you don't? Are you more trustworthy to a friend than a stranger?"

"I still don't see connecting and professionalism as either/or. But I'm weakening."

"Now for the coup de grâs. If your employees were totally professional in all they did, that is, doing whatever it took to fulfill the values of the organization, do you think their customers would have any inkling that company needs actually came before their needs?"

"You're suggesting that the company would sacrifice customer needs if it was necessary for the good of the company."

"Aye. I am. A company would close any division that was losing money no matter what the effect on customers. Customers are only as good as how open their wallets are and how much profit there is to be had."

I had to admit that I have had many buying experiences where I felt I was viewed only as the carrier of a wallet full of credit cards. I nodded my head and said, "I suppose I can agree with that, but it's hardly a master-stoke conclusion."

Angus smiled and raised an index finger in the air. "But I'm only part-way finished. Say Superior Furniture wanted to become more efficient. You told all your employees that competition was getting tougher and costs had to decrease, and productivity had to increase. If everyone knew that company needs came first, would fear of change, including layoffs, race through the halls? Of course. Would employees afraid for their jobs protect their jobs? Of course. Would there be a mad scramble to hide defects and people doing whatever it took to save their own hides? Of course. Would it be different if the company had a well-earned reputation for caring for its employees?"

"So, your point is?"

"Anything that hinders customers and employees from experiencing the 4 Cs reduces the chance of creating loyal customers and staff and anything that enhances the 4 Cs increases the chances. Professionalism reduces connecting and everything else by introducing an artificial barrier to human-to-human contact. Corporate letters and reports are perfect examples of someone trying to be professional by using giant words, convoluted sentences and a lot of pomposity to look professional. What has happened is that the employees who are the most serious, who look the most aloof and formal, appear to others to be the most businesslike, the most professional. These people seem to set the standard, from how to act to how to write. The more formal and official like, the more professional and therefore better. The lady in the yellow at the bowling green was professional and businesslike."

"Point taken. But I see a continuum from professional at one end and anarchy on the other."

"That's how most business decision makers see it. The only way to protect the business is to control the employees. That's the wrong continuum to use."

"The indifference-love continuum, I suppose, should be used to run a business."

"Aye, the ninety-five percent of it that's service. But not that continuum exactly. A better way of understanding employees from the organization's perspective is a very short continuum that starts with good will and ends with mutual well-being. After all, we're hiring wonderful people and should expect a lot more than indifference. The interaction begins with a positive feeling and progresses up from there. Did you notice what Teresa first asked Deanne and Harry?"

"I wondered if we would get back to them. No, I don't recall."

"She asked how their day was. They responded by bringing up how well they connected or didn't connect with their customers. Total honesty too, by the way. Only later were sales brought up. Didn't you find that odd?"

"Yeah, I did. Then I realized it was part of your model and I'd find out what it was all about soon enough."

"I suppose I'm becoming quite transparent. Our target is a loyal employee. What makes them happy is critical. It should not be by having enough free time to play video games. It should not be from a paycheck either. You're renting their time, not their hearts. Primarily, employee happiness should be the result of successfully connecting to customers and contributing to customer well-being and vice versa."

Another penny dropped. "You're saying that employees should get the majority of their job satisfaction from the customer and the organization should get its satisfaction from its employees."

"Exactly."

My head was spinning. "Let me get this straight. I can accept, for the moment, anyway, that an employee can find some satisfaction from the customer's response. However, if I understand you right, you also are saying that the company has employees as customers and somehow…okay, I get it. The company gets 'satisfaction' from happy employees when the employees work hard for the benefit of the organization."

"You don't sound convinced."

"I may be. I want to think this through. In theory, Teresa, my new vice president of happiness, goes around and asks each employee how well they connected with customers that day. Doing that reinforces the importance and benefit of connecting. Right?" I didn't wait for Angus to answer. "It doesn't substitute for the reward of connecting, but it does tell the employees what's really important to the company, the human element." My head was still spinning. "I suppose I can buy that the interaction between an employee and the customer can be rewarding for the employee. I also can buy that employees have human needs that the company can meet, just like employees meet customers' needs. But all this is a lot fuzzier that what we've been discussing up 'till now."

"Right. Our focus should be on the interaction between customer and employee. That's where all the action is. But we also need to look at how the company, the business, supports that interaction. Let's take the buying customer out of the picture. If we make the employee our new customer, the company, and the supervisor, become the new service providers. Does that make sense?"

"Yes. The employee is the customer to the company. The manager represents the company. The employee is the customer to the manager. Got it."

"In our demonstration, Teresa was the service provider, Deanne and Harry were customers. Your company, Superior Furniture was also a service provider because you hired a vice president of happiness and built a very nice staff lounge. Teresa was hired to do the 4 Cs for every employee every day."

"That's clear enough. The company has to recognize the value of the 4 Cs and provide resources, then management has to actually do the 4 Cs."

"Now, you're cooking."

"And you're saying that if the company can get comfortable with near anarchy, that doing the 4 Cs will increase profit."

"That's what I'm saying, except for the anarchy bit."

"Is the employee-manager relationship the same as the customer-employee relationship?"

"Similar enough. If you can do one, you can do the other. But I must add that the employee-manager relationship is a lot more interesting. Often, more often than not, management has to establish virtual customers for many employees."

"Virtual customers?"

Notes

The 4 Cs have to be more important than the bottom-line during Moments of Truth.

Recognizing and admitting mistakes should be a company expectation.

Professionalism dilutes humanism.

Employees are the company.

Good will leads to mutual well-being.

The employee has to initiate the connection with the customer and the company has to initiate the connection with the employee. And, it has to be in an emotional way.

11

Into the Mire of Management

Angus had another question. "What is the role of management?" he asked, totally changing the subject I thought, but waiting for my response this time.

"That's not easy to answer. There are many levels of management with different roles. Executive management must be responsible for the direction of the organization, aware of threats, that sort of thing, while senior management has to translate business objectives into operational terms and provide support for projects and initiatives. Middle managers have to make sure the work gets done."

"And all these levels of management require different skills?"

"I think so. Not everyone can run a business, not

everybody can motivate people. There are a lot of skills involved in running a business."

"Is the top person in the hierarchy, always right?"

"Of course not," I said immediately. I paused to think. Then I realized where he was going. "So, this is where you prove that all businesses are ninety-five percent service."

"Aye."

"Allow me to do that for you. Your point would be to declare that no one in the organization can do everything so everyone in the business has to be connected and coordinated with others for the business to flourish. And people aren't machines, you would say. You can't turn them on and have them do whatever needs to be done. Humans, that is, employees, must be nourished in some way. In the olden days, we used force, now we use regular paychecks. How am I doing so far?"

"Brilliantly—so far."

I held up my index finger. "To continue. Directing people, conducting meetings, how you discuss something in the hallway requires human interaction. And, if that human interaction is a productive one, it has been a service from provider to customer. I would say you are generalizing, but you would say if a person looked at any business, that person would see skills being applied through human interactions. You might conclude by saying that every employee is a customer of other employees and every employee is a service provider to other employees and that is why business is ninety-five percent service."

"George, for someone who is just beginning to look at the 4 Cs of service, you have done a very good job. We would both agree that business relationships are complicated, but would you mind a discussion about employees as customers?"

I was about to answer when he asked another question. "If employees are customers, what do they want from the company?"

"Job security, I think. Good wages. Fair management. Meaningful work. Appreciation, for sure."

"What would be number one?"

"Security, probably."

"According to a study done by your Labor Department some time ago, but the findings are still valid, the top three were feeling appreciated, feeling in on things, and having their personal needs acknowledged."

"So, feeling appreciated is number one?"

"Aye, by quite a bit. Feeling appreciated by their direct supervisor, not some appreciation day put on once a year by the top brass."

"I could have said that, it's Management 101."

"That may be, but in my experience, Management 101 is either forgotten or ignored."

"I guess I have to agree. We forget the simple things. I want to take a closer look at employees as customers. Say this customer wants three things, appreciation, being in on things and having personal needs acknowledged. I'd like to see how the 4 Cs are applied to these needs."

"On the screen?"

"Yes, on the screen."

Angus pushed on the joystick and tapped two buttons. The screen showed Teresa, Deanne and Harry sitting at the same table drinking coffee. It was the same scene as before.

Teresa: Putting down her cup of coffee. "So, Deanne, how was your day?"

Deanne: "Great. Couldn't have been better. I had eight customers, seven of them said 'thank you' about as strongly as it can be said and the eighth one looked me in the eye and said, 'I can't believe the service you people provide in here.'"

Angus stopped the action. "What would you like to see?"

"I don't want to see anything. I want to know what Deanne is feeling."

Angus pushed another button and the scene blurred. Within seven seconds I was feeling a wonderful sense of contentment. There was some excitement to it, and maybe a sense of friendship. I regretted losing the feeling when it faded away. "Would you back up everything and have Teresa asking the question, then stop it?

"Of course." The scene was reset to the beginning.

Teresa: Putting down her cup of coffee. "So, Deanne, how was your day?"

"Stop," I said. "I want to know what Teresa is thinking right now."

Immediately we heard her voice. "Deanne does such great work. It's so enjoyable to talk about how she is doing."

I thought there'd be more about wanting to find out if the sales goals had been met. "Can you go later, when she's asking about sales?" Angus fast-forwarded to that section and we heard Teresa's voice expressing her thoughts.

"This has to be good news for improved volumes. I want this store to increase sales by thirty percent."

"All right," I said. "I was just checking your system. I wasn't sure it was programmed to say anything about making money."

Angus laughed. "Do you know the story of the traveler and the stone masons?"

"Don't think so."

Angus leaned back and looked at the ceiling as if he were seeing the story unfold. "A few hundred years ago, a traveler came across three stone masons chipping away at large blocks of granite. One was sour faced, as though his job was the worst work imaginable. The second was smiling, happy and engaged in his effort. The third was whistling, his arms were a blur; chips were flying everywhere. The traveler asked the first man what he was doing. Relieved to stop a moment, the man said, 'I'm chipping away at this huge block of stone.' The traveler asked the same question of the second man. 'Why, I'm building a wall,' he said. When the third man was asked, he threw his arms out wide and declared, 'I'm helping to create a grand cathedral.' There's a lesson in this story."

"Of course, there is," I agreed.

"The bottom line is, a cathedral is going to be built. Each of those stonemasons is going to contribute. Which one would you like working for you?"

I nodded my head as if I were thinking very hard. "The

first one. I think he is being the most careful and is least likely to make a costly mistake. It also seemed to me that he was concentrating very hard on his work."

Angus ignored my little joke. "The role of management is to ensure that every employee is like the third one. The one working hardest, enjoying his work the most, the one who is most productive and most likely to do whatever it takes to get the job done. And, whom, dare I say," Angus tilted his head down and sideways, so he was looking at me out of the top corners of his eyes, "whom dare I say is the one who is ultimately the most 'professional.'"

"I do believe you have a mean streak somewhere inside you, Angus. I already admitted that a lot of the efforts to be 'professional' tend to make relationships artificial. I get your point. Management must do whatever it can to produce employees like the third guy."

"Which is exactly what we should look at. The ninety-five percent service I've been talking about is in two parts, the organization being set up as a service organization no matter what the business and every employee meeting the needs of his or her customers. Thus, the organization has to provide the 4 Cs to every employee and every employee has to provide the 4 Cs to every other employee."

"That first stonemason you described was me on my first adult job. I was working on an assembly line and all I really thought about was the five feet of dirty, sweaty spot-welding I had to do in a dark noisy place. I was there only for the money."

"Aye. You were in your own world, never really thinking about the product at the end of the line. Tell you what. We should examine what the business should provide every worker."

"Okay. I'm game for that."

"Before we get into that, we need to look more at who the employee-customers of the business are, what they want, and how to provide it, just like employees have to do with their customers."

"Of course. What about virtual customers?" I asked, curious what he meant by that.

"Ah, yes. I forgot. We'll get to them too."

Notes

Feeling appreciated is the primary reward for most workers.

An important outcome, one of many, is for the business to make money.

The primary role of management is making sure every employee is emotionally engaged in his/her work.

Being professional does not lie in formality. It is the ability to succeed efficiently.

12

Build a Great Team

Angus turned to the console and quickly pressed half a dozen buttons. The screen came alive with a soccer game. Our view was from the nosebleed section of the packed stands. We could see the soccer field ringed with what looked like a hundred thousand cheering fans. "You're probably not a football fan," he said, "but I should expand your concept of what football really is. In our game of football, we use our feet. What a concept, eh, football played with the feet? I want to show you four things. Watch."

I watched. I understand the game; keep kicking a ball back and forth between two teams until someone kicks it into a net. The usual score is something like one, zero. How exciting. The crowd noise picked up. I watched one player in green make a quick arm gesture to another player in green before he kicked the ball to him.

"That's number one of the four things and, oh, number two," Angus said. "Keep watching."

I shrugged my shoulders and kept watching. The guy who had received the pass was running downfield pushing the ball in front of him. Suddenly, he kicked it far to his left. Another player in green swooped in and without stopping kicked the ball into the opposing goal. The crowd went wild. The players in green jumped up and down and hugged one another. Some tore off their shirts and waved them like flags as they ran along the sidelines. Fans began streaming onto the field.

"And that's numbers three and four," he said as he clicked off the screen. "What did you notice?"

"I noticed the players were kicking the ball rather than carrying it. No, seriously, the green team evidently won the game. It was probably overtime since it was sudden death. It was an important game; the stands were packed. The players were obviously very good. I noticed they scored using a play I learned in basketball, the give and go. My guess it was a professional game. And I would guess it was probably a championship game. How'd I do?"

"Very well. You mentioned all the elements I wanted you to notice. You're right, it was a professional game and a championship game too, although altered somewhat for research purposes. Neither team is a real team but based on two very popular ones. What you saw contained all the critical elements of a great team, something all businesses should have, but few actually do.

A few years back, maybe ten by now, I had the pleasure of meeting another of you Yanks at a conference in Vancouver,

British Columbia, Canada, a wonderful place. He was and still is an organizational development expert; Dr. Rudy Williams. He had this model of a team that I thought was brilliant."

Angus got up and walked over to the white board and wiped it clean with a cloth. He then wrote:

Compelling Task	Sense of Membership
Personal Reward	Influence on the Team

Angus continued while standing at the board, "Rudy calls it the Four-Part Teaming model and it makes all the sense in the world. Look at the upper left quadrant. The footballers had a compelling task, playing to win the championship. Now look at the lower left. Each had a personal reward. These players are paid grand salaries and bonuses, they have fans chasing after them like they were rock stars, you get the picture. Lower right quadrant. They each had influence on the team like calling a play in the middle of the action, discussing how to do things at practice, that sort of thing. And for a sense of membership on a team on the upper right, how can you miss their uniforms, their colors, working out together and everyone knowing of the others' important contributions?

The primary task of an organization is to get organized. The Four-Part Teaming model may be the best way to do that. The compelling task for the higher-ups is running a successful business. But as you know, that isn't enough for most employees. Of the four parts, I believe the compelling task is the most powerful because it must arise from a compelling vision. It is amazing to me what people can do when the vision is a supercharged one, like creating a grand cathedral or winning a championship. Which of the four are most relevant varies with different circumstances and cultures. All of them are necessary.

Employees want to feel in on things but for the most part, that isn't enough. They also must know that they have some influence on what happens. Reward? It isn't just a paycheck. A sense of membership may be the weakest area for most companies. Oh, some may give away T-shirts every once in a while, but membership is more than just a uniform. It's working together to accomplish something important to them, sacrificing for the good of all, being acknowledged by those inside and outside the organization that they are contributing member of a great team. Watch this."

Angus went back to the console and the green team locker room came into focus. Players were pouring champagne over each other, embracing one another, shouting in each other's face, all those things that happen in a victor's locker room. One was empting a bottle over another's back while screaming "Agggghhhh," when Angus stopped the action and we heard his thoughts, "You were the hero today mate, I'm proud to be on the team with you." The scene blurred.

Euphoria came over me. It was a combination of joy, relief, giddiness, maybe even love. I was envious. I'd never experienced such a thrill of victory. I'd seen winning locker rooms before, but only while sitting in front of the television and while I was reaching for more potato chips. I've experienced success, but nothing like this.

Angus interrupted my thoughts. "Wouldn't that be a great way of ending the workday?"

I looked wide-eyed at Angus. "That was something."

"You get that feeling only from overcoming a significant challenge. We were talking this morning about hope and that there is a degree of anxiety when you connect human-to-human. One of the payoffs of that anxiety is some of what you just felt. When you team up with others, hopes increase, dependency on others increases, the risk increases, the outcome becomes bigger. The reward, however, is well worth it."

"I can see that if a company did more with team building, employees could become more engaged. But I'm not sure any business can have as compelling a goal as winning a soccer championship. Sports is different than working nine to five."

"Only in degree, not in effect." Angus fiddled with the console again. This time the scene was a fish market. There was a long display of fresh fish. Behind the display was a man in an apron, obviously the fish seller. Talking to him was another man wearing a top coat.

Man in topcoat:	"Fred, you know that salmon you sold me last week, the one you recommended so highly?"
Fish seller:	"Yes. How did you like it?"
Man in topcoat:	"I'm here to tell you it was the best fish I ever tasted."

The scene blurred. I knew what was coming. Then it

came. A warm glow. Love between the two men? I'm not sure. Euphoria? Almost. Contentment, absolutely.

Angus paused the machine. "There is no reason why most employees cannot end most workdays feeling what you just felt."

"By the organization setting up a great team using the four-part teaming model?"

"Of course. May I use Superior Furniture as an example of how to do that?"

I figured what was coming and wanted to short-circuit his intent. "You mean, may you use Superior Furniture as an example of how not to do that."

"It may be that you're doing better than you think."

"Somehow, I doubt that. Fire away."

"I assume Superior Furniture has a vision statement. What is it?"

"Superior Furniture will be the largest furniture chain east of the Mississippi."

"Uh, huh. Wonderful. Do you have a mission statement?"

"Superior Furniture will sell quality furniture at the lowest price with superior customer service."

"What do you think was the vision of the football team I just showed you?"

"I don't know. Something like win the championship?"

"It was 'be the best football team in the world.' Which vision statement would get your blood flowing more, yours or the football team's?"

"Ours is pretty dull."

"Clipping toenails would be more exciting."

Ouch. That one stung, but I continued. "So the compelling

goal begins with vision and mission statements?"

"It begins there, right you are. But there is more. Even the most exciting vision cannot always trickle down to every employee. The less direct impact an employee has on making the vision a reality, the more other statements have to be found that more directly engage these workers. Divisions of a corporation can have vision and mission statements and so can smaller teams all the way down to work units. These statements must support the company's statement, of course, but they must sing to those it is intended for.

I know one group within a large organization whose mission was to be the 'best in customer service and the rest of the company will know it.' This prompted them to work hard at both providing a great service and to find ways of tooting their own horn. That compelled them to do a good job since they were advertising their results. That was a compelling goal for that team, let me tell you. I worked with a hospital pharmacy once whose mission was, 'Right drug, right patient, on time, every time.' They too were highly motivated to never let a mistake happen."

"You're using vision and mission statements almost interchangeably. Aren't they different?"

"Technically, yes. A vision statement is about a future state and is usually quite visual or may I say visceral and is best when it is short and concise. A mission statement is often longer and describes more clearly how things will get done. My point is that an emotionally engaging vision or mission statement of less than a dozen words has great effect and is the only way an employee can remember what the real goal is. You want to inspire the workers, enable them to focus on the ultimate goal, and maybe most important, include them in its construction. I recommend gathering a team together and creating a vision. In a very good way, it both defines a compelling task and gives each employee influence over the team. It contributes to a sense of membership and partly defines personal rewards. Can you imagine not doing this?"

Ruefully, I could imagine not doing this. Superior Furniture never did it, nor did anywhere else I worked. But what an advantage such team building would give any company that did. I thought back to my childhood team experiences. We had a joy of belonging together, even if it was a ragtag group of boys with our only uniform a faded baseball cap. Winning the game was such a big deal. I remembered the shock the first time we turned a double play in a real game just like we had worked on in practice.

"Can you see how the 4 Cs are involved in the process of creating a work unit vision statement?" Angus asked.

After just a moment's thought, I could see that. "Working as a team to create a team vision seems like all 4 Cs. The organization is connecting human-to-human by allowing the process to occur and putting emphasis on a compelling goal. It is contributing in at least two ways, informing the workers of the goal and certainly respecting their input in defining it. Confirming comes with the workers agreeing on the vision statement. And I can see collaborating being included just by doing the process."

Angus smiled. "Powerful stuff, eh?"

I thought so. The amount of time and energy businesses spend on mechanical processes far outweighs the attention it spends on human interaction. There we seem to let nature takes it course. We tout the importance of input from line workers and then ignore them.

Notes

Great teams require a compelling goal, a sense of membership on the team, individual influence on the team and personal rewards for being on the team.

Employee-created vision statements, especially at the work unit level, are worth every ounce of effort it takes to create them.

Most managers pay far more attention to machines and processes than they do to people.

13

Personal Mission Statements

My thoughts drifted. "You got me thinking about when I was a kid. When I was young, my dad used to take me to this neighborhood barbershop. There was only one chair, the owner was the only guy in the place. I loved going there, sitting with all the men, listening to what they had to say, glancing through the hunting magazines, then when my turn came, being fussed over, treated like one of the guys, and otherwise loving every moment of the haircut morning.

Talk about value streams, this guy's barbershop was one heck of a moment of truth value stream. Every moment for me in there was great. The smells, the magazines, everything. Then, the owner added a second chair. The new barber wasn't an owner but an employee. I'm sure there was a period of adjustment as we got used to him, but things were never the same. When the owner wasn't there it was much different. The other guy didn't talk as much, seemed to rush through haircuts, just didn't put the same attitude or care into what he was doing."

"Aye, ownership makes all the difference," Angus said, nodding his head. Then surprisingly, he let me continue.

"That's right. What a clear difference between owner and employee. The owner, with direct contact with his customers, was reinforced directly by them. And his expectations were met directly too. He could take the money, have a clean shop, close when he wanted to, all those things that make owning the business worthwhile. While the employee is actually one step removed. He gets a paycheck rather than money from the customer and is not directly able to meet the expectations of his customers; at least he has to get agreement from the owner maybe on how to do it or do what the owner tells him to do. I'm not sure what I'm trying to say here. Maybe that when the owner meets the customers' expectations, he is more rewarded than when his employee meets the customers' expectations."

"Yer'r on to a delightful new subject, making employees act like owners, a goal of management since the days of the pharaohs. Keep talking."

I kept talking. Maybe I could teach Angus a thing or two. "The reward from customer service is, I think, automatically different for the owner. And, I think this is true too; the larger the organization, the less reward there is for employees along the customer value stream and the more chance there is of negative moments of truth for the employee."

Angus shook his head. "Too abstract. I don't know what

you're saying."

"Okay. Let's take Superior Furniture. The billing department. They have a moment of truth with every key stroke. Either the information is correct on the bill or it isn't. But they never see the customer. How can they be engaged in the 4 Cs when the customer is only a name and number on a sheet of paper? How can employees get rewarded like owners when they never see a customer?"

"Aye, that's exactly why we need to be figuring out something that will be great for both customer and employee. That's where the organization really needs to know the expectations of its employees, so they can meet them since the customer won't be able to."

"Yes. In a one-person operation like the barbershop and the newsagents, feedback from the customer is immediate and direct, if the owner has open eyes and ears. If they don't, they're out of business. Once past that direct contact and, I should add, direct consequences, things become fuzzy. In the two-person barbershop, the second guy was not directly affected by not meeting anyone's expectations as long as he met the boss's needs."

Angus tilted his head. "Would you say that again?"

"Be glad to," I held up my finger for emphasis ala Angus. "This is Corbett's corollary. The more removed from the consequences of failing to meet a customer's expectations, the less likely an employee is to meet them unless something is done to enhance the reward for doing so. Furthermore, I don't think I have ever used the word 'furthermore' in conversation before. Furthermore, if the employee's reward for meeting customer expectation is tied to his or her own expectations, the more likely everyone's expectations will be met."

"That's why we need virtual customers."

"I knew we would eventually get to that."

"But first, I'd like to go back to your barbershop. Each time the barber snipped with his scissors, there was a moment of truth, as we described it. He either did it right or cut too short or not short enough. The same is true of the shop's employee and of your billing people. Each time they did their detailed task, it was good for the customer or bad for the customer. Is that what you mean? I want to make sure."

Uh oh. Angus had that tone of voice again. Where were we headed this time? "Yes, that is exactly what I mean. And the only difference between them is distance from the customer. That and one person being the owner." I had to add that quickly because I figured Angus was going to make a huge point of the difference between being an owner and being an employee. "And we've been sorting-out how all this relates to employee loyalty."

"We have. First though, we have to define what our ideal employee looks like—and you already know that."

I hate it when he does that. I thought back over what we had discussed. "The woman in the green sweater."

"Aye, but we'll need more detail than a green sweater, but you're going in the right direction. Why don't I go down and make some tea? While I do that, use the white board and describe what you think is the ideal employee. From that, we can construct a virtual customer." Without waiting for my answer as usual, he got up and went down the stairs. I was left sitting in my chair wondering exactly what I was supposed to do.

I had a lot of prior conceptions of what an ideal employee was, but from what we had talked about today, I had to put something entirely new together. Plus, my brain was getting tired. This was a lot of new material, much of it contrary to what I had previously believed. The 4 Cs was simple. That was attractive. I was impressed with the computer. I was anxious to get back to work to try things out. So, I sat pondering for a while, until I heard the kettle whistling. I scooted over to the board and wrote this:

Ideal Employee
1. Hired based on job competency and customer service personality.
2. Knows and acts upon the 4 Cs.
3. Enjoys an interesting and challenging job and feels appreciated.
4. Ends most days with a sense of satisfaction and meaningful contribution.

I read my list over a few times and was satisfied with what I had written. But of course, Angus would have a pointed comment or two. He arrived carrying a fully laden tray that wobbled as he walked, almost capsizing twice. It was filled with small cakes spread around a three-tiered cake caddie (I think that's what they're called), a silver tea service and old-fashioned hand-painted teacups and saucers. Angus busied himself setting out the cakes and cups, asked if I took milk and poured that into my cup before filling it with tea. Only when we had a bite of cake did he look up at the board. He gestured toward the board with the hand that held a half-eaten cake.

"Brilliant. Exactly what I would have put down…"

I knew the tone of voice. The "yes-but" inflection. "But…?" I asked.

"I would have added a number five. 'Has defined personally meaningful vocational goals.' You see, that's where the need of a virtual customer begins."

I took another bite of what Angus said was an empire biscuit, two round biscuit type things with iced topping and jam filling. "That makes sense. We have to tie what the employee wants from the job with what they can get. What they should want and get is customer appreciation." I thought for a moment as I finished chewing the empire biscuit. "I suppose that's the problem, most employees don't get customer appreciation. At least in any meaningful way."

Angus reached over to the computer console and punched a few buttons. "We should look at a typical employee. Any preferences?"

I wanted to be creative and come up with someone who does customer service but rarely sees a customer. "Let's see a woman who cleans rooms in a hotel."

Angus did more maneuvers on the console and the screen lit up with a woman pushing a cleaning cart down what looked like a hotel hallway. Our view was from the front, she was walking toward us.

"Susan," Angus said. The woman lifted her head as if her name had been called by a good friend. "Why do you work at the hotel?"

Her pleasant expression didn't change. "Oh, hello, professor. To pay me bills like everyone else."

"If you didn't have to work, would you keep your job?"

"Like if I won the football pools? No fear. I'd be home before me mop hit the floor."

Susan began collecting the supplies she'd need for the next room.

"What do you think of the hotel customers?"

"Some leave tips, most don't. I rarely see them, so I don't think much about them. But some leave such an awful mess, you wonder what they do at home."

"Thank you, Susan."

"Ta," she said as she entered the next room.

"Hold on, I'd like to ask her some questions."

"Oh. Sorry, George. I was going to explain my point." Angus moved the joystick and Susan appeared back at her cart, looking at us expectantly.

"Susan, I'd like to know what motivates you to do your job."

She looked at me like I was a complete idiot. I felt uncomfortable even though she was just an image on a screen. A computer-generated image at that.

"Well, sir…"

Angus interrupted. "His name is George Corbett."

"Well, Mr. Corbett," she continued. "What motivates me to do my job is that I wouldn't have it if I didn't do it. The manager inspects the rooms regularly and the customers certainly would complain if I did a bad job of it."

"Do you get thanked when you do a good job?"

Susan smiled. "Some people leave tips. That's always good, but I do the job the same way in every room. So they're just being nice."

Suddenly the image froze. I knew what was coming.

Almost immediately I heard Susan's voice, "Must be some management type sent here to motivate us. The jobs some blighters have. They'd learn a whole lot more if they just did the work for a day. That would be the right way to go about it."

"Want to continue?" Angus asked.

"I have a couple of more questions for Susan, if you don't mind getting out of her head."

"Righto."

The image unfroze and Susan stood waiting for the next question.

"Susan, besides a paycheck, at the end of the day, what makes you believe you did a good job?"

She thought for a minute. "I do what I'm told. I do each room like I'm supposed to. I don't get any demerits."

"Do you get any joy from your work?" I knew that was a dumb question as soon as it came out. I'm glad Angus didn't switch the computer to show thoughts.

"Joy? You must be joking. Cleaning a joy?" She paused. "I suppose I do like a clean room. That's satisfying, to take a mess and make it right."

"Thank you, Susan," Angus said as he turned off the screen. "I wanted to stop it here so we could talk about what Susan represents. To me, she is a typical employee, removed from the customers and doing a job that, in itself, is not what we would call inspiring. Would you agree?"

"Absolutely. Most people have jobs like that. A lot of work, little customer contact, and not what they would be doing if they didn't have to earn a living."

"And they are exactly the people we need to make ideal employees. The question is, how do we get them to exhibit the five things we declared make the ideal employee."

I nodded my head. "Tough question—and let me guess, the answer is a virtual customer."

"Exactly."

"So, what is a virtual customer?"

"I'll have Susan show you." Angus went back to the console, diddled with some buttons and the screen showed Susan wheeling her cart down the hall, this time away from us. Angus stopped her in her tracks. "The only difference between how she was before and how she is now is a virtual customer I created for her."

This was going to be interesting, a virtual customer for a virtual employee.

"Susan," Angus said.

She stopped and turned around to look at us. "Yes?"

"Does your hotel have a vision statement?"

She smiled. "Oh, yes. 'We will be a haven that every guest will return to as a friend.'"

"What does that mean?"

"Well, we treat people so well they feel that they belong here, like a friend staying at the house a wee while."

I had a question. "Susan, does that vision affect how you do things?"

"Ach, aye. Totally. In me old job, it was just cleaning rooms. Now I understand that these are people I'm helping, like they could be friends once we got to know one another. I make up their rooms as if they were staying in my own home, which in a way they are. I like the idea of creating a wee haven for people. The world can be a rough place. I can do my bit to make it better."

"Thank you, Susan. Sorry to hold you up."

"Cherrio," Susan said, before turning and pushing her cleaning cart down the hall.

"Let's follow her into the next room," Angus suggested.

Susan reached a door on the left side of the hall and softly knocked. She waited a moment, knocked again, said, "Housekeeping," then unlocked the door and went inside. We followed.

The room was a mess. The bed was practically stripped of its linens. Towels were draped over chairs, dropped on the floor and hung on doorknobs. Pages of a newspaper were strewn everywhere. The dresser top was cluttered with candy wrappers, empty cups, full ashtrays, half a dozen empty cans and a number of paper bags.

The action stopped as Susan was on her way into the bathroom.

"My, oh my," she thought, "I'll have a time getting this room ready for the next folk to use it."

"Let's jump ahead twenty minutes," Angus said. He moved the joystick and pushed a couple of buttons.

The scene changed to Susan opening the door to leave the room. It was sparkling. The image blurred.

Within seconds my mind went back twenty years, to when I was promoted manager of one of our stores. It was a feeling I hadn't felt in a while. Contentment. Pride. Accomplishment. The sense of a job well done. When the feeling faded, I was still smiling. It made all the sense in the world. If the employee can't go to the customer, have the customer come to the employee. That's what the company vision is, a virtual customer. It's an image you can carry with you, bring out after every task and give yourself immediate feedback.

"I get it," I said to Angus.

"I can see that," he said. "Of course, it gets a bit complicated."

"Of course."

"The boss is a customer too, you know, as are co-workers and the worker is a customer to herself as well."

"Sure," I said, waiting for the Angus Express to express itself.

"The boss is an exacting customer. Employees are told what to do and how well they're doing it. This can be bad if done poorly, but when done well, the boss provides clear expectations so workers can measure how well they're succeeding. Clear goals are necessary to enjoy a sense of accomplishment and when paired with appreciation, are a great motivating combination. When expectations are clear, accountability also becomes clear and co-workers become customers. Susan wants to keep up her end to please her boss, to support her co-workers, to satisfy herself and, naturally, make customers feel like friends."

I held up my hand. "Angus, before you go on, could I talk with Susan again?" I no more than asked when Susan appeared on the screen. She was standing in a hallway chatting with another housekeeper.

"Susan, may I interrupt?"

She turned to look at me. "Of course. Oh, hello Mr. Corbett. It's good to see you again. What can I do for you?"

It felt good to be remembered. Then I realized this was all computer animation. "Ah, Susan, last time I was here, you told us the hotel vision. Now I think that every employee of every business also has a vision or maybe a mission of why they work. For example, some people work at their job because it is the only job they could find, and they have to pay their bills. Some people work only to pay for a car. That sort of thing. Does that make sense?"

"Aye, it makes sense. You're asking what my personal mission statement is. We've done that here. All of us. My mission here is to create a haven for our guests that I am personally proud of. I work because I have too, Lord knows. But having to work does nothing with my attitude about my job. When it was just a job, I treated it that way, and myself too. Work was a drudge to get over as quickly as possible. Then we worked on the vision for the hotel, and later our own mission statements. Things began to make much more sense. I wasn't here just to work, I was here to accomplish something important. Realizing that made all the difference."

"Wow."

"Aye, wow, indeed." Susan started shaking her finger at me, almost scolding. "You listen to the professor, he knows what he's talking about." I looked over at Angus, who was grinning. "I had to throw that in, just for effect." The screen went blank.

Notes

If the customer is not available to say "thank you," the company vision, manager and co-workers have to be extremely good substitutes.

Clear goals for employees are a must.

Know and reinforce every one of your employees' personal mission statements.

The ideal employee has job competency and customer service personality; knows and acts upon the 4 Cs; enjoys an interesting and challenging job and feels appreciated; is pursuing personally meaningful goals and ends most days with a sense of contribution.

14

Virtual Customers

This was good stuff. "Angus, this is all making great sense to me now."

"Is it?"

"Yes. Immediate feedback is one of the core concepts to efficiency and I see how the organization has to figure out how to give employees quick, effective and rewarding customer feedback especially when the customers are not directly available. Having a clear vision and mission allows each employee to judge immediately if they are doing the right thing. And the more this is from the customer's perspective, the better."

"Aye, that's true…" Angus nodded his head, but had a far-away look in his eyes.

Man, there he goes again, I thought. "But…?"

"I wonder who is the best one to give the employee feedback, the boss or the customer."

I thought for a moment or two. This could be a trick. It has to be the customer. Why would he ask? "The customer?"

"Aye, but from whom do most employees get feedback?"

"The boss."

"Usually, and usually in the form of correcting mistakes. And while we're at it, who do you suppose knows the least about how well an employee is doing?"

With some resignation I shrugged my shoulders. "The boss?"

"Who do you suppose knows most about how well an employee is doing?"

"Not the boss?"

"Co-workers. They know if the job is being done well or not. Few employees, however, can give and receive feedback for the good of all. What happens in most places is resentment of someone not doing the job well, talking behind their backs, snide comments and the like. Some complain to the boss or third parties to triangulate the problem and further disrupt healthy and honest communication."

"And you, dear sir, have the solution."

"George, it should be clear by now. If everyone in the organization recognizes that he or she is a customer to someone, and provides customer service to others, everyone is aware of knowing who their customers are, what they want and how to provide it, no matter who that customer is, a paying customer, a co-worker, a boss or themselves. Remember the importance of the fourth C, the customer being sincerely asked for feedback, being given permission as it were to complain?

That's the core of great customer service, great staff satisfaction and, ultimately, a successful business. Let's take a look at how it works." Angus turned and stabbed at a couple of buttons.

The screen lit up, but barely. I could see flashes of light and maybe a few shadows, but I couldn't tell what was on the screen.

"Bit lighter, please," Angus said.

The screen lit up enough so I could tell we were in some kind of mine.

"I didn't know you could do that."

"Of course, why not? 'Let there be light.'"

"Hey, Joe." Our attention went back to the screen. There were two men stripped to the waste, covered with grime in what I guessed was a coal mine. The man nearby was calling to the other one.

The other one stopped and turned, "Yeah?"

"Joe, we've got a problem."

"Yeah, what's that?"

"You're not up to speed with the drilling and I have to slow down. Means we won't make quota."

Angus stopped the action. "What do you think Joe is going to say?"

I smiled. "Depends on how you set the computer. Did you push the bottom customer service button or one or two or even three?"

Angus chuckled. "For your information, I pushed the bottom button."

"Then Joe is going to tell the other guy to get stuffed."

Angus pushed the joystick.

Joe responded. "You try working with this bloomin' drill and see how you come off."

"Okay," I asked, "What happens when one of the good buttons is pushed?"

Angus pushed the second button and moved the joystick a bit.

Joe responds again. "I'm sorry, Al. I don't seem to have it today."

"Press all the buttons." The image reversed for an instant, then Joe responded again.

"Al, you're right, I'm lagging today. Sorry. Might be better if we switched jobs for a bit, maybe I can get me rhythm back. What would you think about doing that, or mate, I'm all ears if you have a better idea."

"Well, Joe, since you put it that way, I think I do have a better idea. You've been slow the last couple of days. At first, I thought maybe you were hung over or something. Are you feeling okay?"

Joe shakes his head. "No, I don't feel good at all."

"That's what I thought. Why don't you shut down and see the nurse topside, get checked out? I don't want to catch what you have, and I don't want anyone else to get it either. You look a mess."

Joe laughs. "You're probably right."

Angus shut down the screen. "You see how they connected human to human, contributed to each other and confirmed? They watched out for each other and the business. Perfect, if I don't say so myself."

"I see that. Joe, although he is lagging and causing Al some problems, has become Al's customer. And as soon as Al says something to Joe, Al becomes Joe's customer. As they talk, the company becomes a customer to both of them. Interesting. No boss got involved either."

"Actually, the boss and the company are involved by the specificity of the goals that have been set and the accountability of Al and Joe to reach them. Al was able to say something and do so very clearly because he and Joe were not making their quota. It wasn't simply Al's opinion, but acknowledging a negative behavior that was affecting their productivity."

"Is all this involved in identifying what a virtual customer is?"

Angus paused for a moment, his eyebrows nearly pressed together as he thought. "Aye. We talked about everyone being a customer, including the company and we talked about the company vision and a bit about personal mission statements. Aye, time to talk about how a virtual customer ties everything together."

"I'm glad of that." I looked at my watch. It was almost five o'clock. I had been there for seven hours. "I've enjoyed my day, but I should be going soon, and I can't take up much more of your time. You have been more than generous."

"You are most welcome. So, ready to define the virtual customer?"

"Ready."

"A virtual customer is how the organization has designed its customer service culture. It's how much each employee believes that the fundamental accountability for all employees is excellent customer service to all customers."

"That's a bit abstract, Angus. I thought you'd have created

some mental mockup of a customer that you somehow injected into people."

Angus' eyes widened in mock surprise. "But I have."

I looked at him with my best questioning look.

"What do you get if you combine energy, caring and openness, and the 4 Cs, add an inspiring vision statement, toss in a personal mission statement, flavor with everyone being a customer to everyone and immediate feedback freely given and accepted by all?"

"A Labrador Retriever?"

Angus ignored my comment. "Close your eyes." I closed my eyes. "Imagine," he said, "you are crawling across burning sands, weak from thirst, your throat is raw and dry. The air is as hot as an oven and the sun is blistering your skin. Got that image?"

"Yes. It's what I feel like playing golf." I opened my eyes.

"Keep your eyes closed. Imagine again crawling on that hot sand. Sand in your eyes, your nose and down your throat."

"Got it," I said, my eyes closed.

"What are you feeling?"

"Hot and thirsty."

"Good. Now imagine a waiter suddenly appearing carrying a tray holding a pitcher of ice water and a glass. Take the glass and let him fill it to overflowing. Drink it down. Let the water cascade over your face. Drink deep and long. How do you feel now?"

"Great."

"That first feeling of need and that second feeling of relief is the virtual customer."

I had no idea what he meant. "You need to explain that a

whole lot more for me to understand what you're talking about."

"I shall. By hiring the right people, providing the right inspiration, following the right values and reinforcing service, an organization creates in its employees a response to a customer so visceral that it is like going from an overwhelming need to a sublime contentment."

"Keep talking."

"Ideally, employees who are customer driven are actually uncomfortable, not quite dying of thirst maybe, but physically discombobulated when someone has a need. They are driven to meet that need and once they do, enjoy a rewarding sense of well-being. This internal drive is what I'm calling a virtual customer. It isn't a pretend customer. It's a real feeling of commitment to help another. Mark my words, it's either there or it isn't, like being pregnant. Once it's there, you can count on the employee doing a great job most of the time, as often as humanly possible."

"Now, let me make sure we're thinking the same thing. You're saying that this virtual customer thing exits or should exist for people doing customer service. Are you also saying that the same thing applies to managers for their employees?"

"Absolutely yes."

"So, you want employees to treat all their customers, paying customers, co-workers, bosses and whoever else with this virtual customer drive thing and for bosses to also be driven by an internal virtual customer, namely their employees?"

"Absolutely yes, again."

"But you said you have to hire for it, and I don't think

there are enough living people like that to go around."

"Rarely can you hire someone who is ready to do the work the best way immediately no matter what the job and who the candidate. There is the organization culture to adjust to if nothing else. But, once you have hired wisely, there has to be sufficient understanding of what is expected and even better feedback and reinforcement. You can succeed with any decent hire, but you must be willing to pay the cost of development. Naturally, you pay one way or the other. Wise organizations pay the costs of service enlightenment; poor ones pay to correct mistakes."

"My guess is that's a large investment up front to create service enlightenment."

"Aye. At the very least, you need a leader who has vision, at least one manager who manages with the 4 Cs and at least one front line staff who is driven to provide great customer service. You identify and quantify what they do, define expectations for everyone, then reinforce like crazy. You reward the good and get rid of the bad. You have to have role models, nothing works in the abstract. Theory doesn't produce results, actions do. The best way is to simply point and say, 'This is how it's done.'

Now you ken that employees do what the boss measures. The boss isn't the final customer, but the boss is the customer employees respond to most of the time. The mentality of many employees is a 'have to' mentality, not the strongest nor the most beneficial way of motivating someone. You want the boss to emphasize the 4 Cs. No, more than that. You want the boss to be the 4 Cs. You want the boss to measure the 4 Cs, to model the 4 Cs, to reward the 4 Cs." Angus shook his head.

"There are so many ways to do this poorly."

"You've made it clear that employees have to internalize the emotions of what customer service is. I suppose that's so the same drive is there all the time no matter what kind of customer; how important, internal or external, co-worker or boss."

Angus reached for the teapot resting under a blue tea cozy. "Would you like some more tea?"

"No, thanks."

"I'll just pour myself a wee cup." Angus poured a bit of milk into his cup, added the tea and sat back in his chair. "The idea of a virtual customer is important. The employee, any and all of them from top to bottom and from one side to the other, must perceive everyone who has an expectation of them to be a customer. This must be automatic, as automatic as a give-and-go in football. You don't think about it, you just do it." Angus sighed. "I wish I had a better name for it. The virtual customer is like a biological drive, a 'must-do' that is hard to stop. If you feel it and don't respond to it, you feel awful. That's how it should be."

"I think 'virtual customer' is a great name. You want all employees to have the concept in the front of their brains. Having the image of a virtual customer in your mind is a lot better than memorizing a dozen or more service standards."

"What is the image of a virtual customer you have in your mind?"

"It's actually not an image at all. It's more of a feeling of contributing on a human level. I guess I really like the concept of connecting human-to-human. That resonated with me when you said it. I thought about my dad and me connecting when we'd play catch, go fishing, that sort of thing. The barbershop. That memory really made it clear. And I liked your vice president of happiness. What a great thing for employees, to know that they're vitally important, respected, encouraged, that what they think and feel counts. That's a lot different than most HR departments. You know, we used to tell our sales force to treat our customers like they were our grandmothers. I suppose that's the same idea as a virtual customer."

"Did it work?"

"Not really."

"An idea like that, or any abstract concept doesn't have the same effect as a feeling. You have to do what you can to create that feeling. This is along the line of John Kotter's "see-feel-change" model. Intellectual motivation from facts, figures, standards and the like is nothing compared to a sensory reaction. That's part of the power behind the computer images. They are so real they help create an emotional reaction, much different that you would get watching a slide presentation of the same material."

I was immediately embarrassed thinking about the number of slide presentations I've made listing all our customer service ideas. How could I have ever thought that lists on slides illuminated on a screen in a dark room to a dozen half-asleep people would have any impact? We did role-plays to help our staff learn, but I can see how lame that was too. We had the completely wrong idea. It is not what you teach; it's who you are and how you relate to everyone else. What I didn't realize was that if you have an objective, like selling something or reciting a script, you automatically put up a barrier to connecting human-to-human. "You know," I said to Angus,

"I'm embarrassed at how much I relied on scripts. I see your point now of how useless they are."

Angus sat up in his chair to put down his teacup. "Actually, scripts are fine once you have a virtual customer in your head."

"What?"

"Sure. Once you have the right emotional perspective, scripts are useful for organizational consistency as I said and are handy in unusual or tough situations, so you don't have to rely just on quick thinking to make things turn out right."

"Are they preferred?"

"No, no. The anarchy you mentioned earlier is preferable to reciting lines." Angus leaned forward to make his next point. "The more rules you add and the further from what is perceived as direct customer reinforcement they are, the harder it is for employees to be happy doing what they do. Some of the feeling is personality, of course, which is why we hire for that, but most of it is determined every day by how they are treated. But our goal is for every employee to end every day happy. You get that only by everyone expressing the 4 Cs to every one else."

"A real, top to bottom service culture."

"Aye, a true service culture."

Notes

Co-workers provide effective feedback, second only to customers.

Wise organizations invest in learning, poor ones pay for mistakes.

A virtual customer is the emotionally internalized combination of the company vision, the employee mission and the customer's hopes.

15

A True Service Culture

Angus and I talked for a while longer about customer service mentality. He even used his super computer to show me two training videos, "FISH," about a fish market in Seattle where employee play was emphasized and another called "It's a Dog's World" that compared the care a dog received from his veterinarian and what his human owner got through the typical medical system. All of it meshed with the 4 Cs extraordinarily well. But I still didn't have a good handle on what I should be doing when I got back. The theory sounded great, but the how wasn't clear. What was the best way for me to change our organization? So, I asked the critical question.

"How much would you charge for your super computer?" As Angus let the bemused look on his face disappear, I

161

continued. "Okay, maybe Superior Furniture can't afford a super computer to teach how to create a service culture. So how can we get ourselves to where we should be?"

Angus looked at the clock then reached out his hand to touch my forearm. "George, do you have time for a wee deoch en doris?"

For about the fiftieth time I had no idea what he was talking about. "I don't know. How long does a wee deoch en doris take?"

He tapped my forearm. "A bit of whisky my friend. How about a wee dram while we put everything together?"

We reassembled in the sitting room where Angus prepared our drinks. He came over to my chair carrying a small tray with two empty glasses, a small pitcher of water and a half-full carafe of what I guessed was the whisky.

"This, George, is the water of life, my absolute favorite, ten-year old Laphroaig. It's made on the Isle of Islay off the west coast of Scotland. It's a bit harsh so if you will permit me, I'll add what I think is the proper amount of water. He handed me a glass, now half filled with the water/whisky mix. "Try to taste the flavors, peat, smoke, seaweed, maybe a bit of iodine."

Iodine, seaweed, smoke, peat? This must be the Scottish liquid equivalent of haggis. I took a sip. Acid laced with broken glass etched my throat. I choked but held it down. "Ah, yes, iodine," I croaked. I took another sip, choked again, and held it down again. "And peat, got that, maybe a bit of seaweed, too." I held up the glass and smiled weakly.

Angus took a sip of his drink. "Aye, it is good isn't it. But now to explain how satisfied customers and happy staff come together. It all starts with the organization. The company must have an engaging vision and translate that vision as many ways as needed so everyone in the organization is emotionally engaged in one form or other of the vision. Few companies do that. As much as possible, every employee should be part of creating a vision statement, especially at the department or work unit level. Once this is done, when new employees are hired, enough time must be spent welcoming them as active team members in fulfilling the team's vision. They must know, though the four-part teaming model how important the task is, what their membership to the team means, what rewards there are and how they will have continuing influence. You must not skimp on doing this.

The company must make it clear to every employee that employees come first, that they are the business and the organization will do everything in its power to provide the 4 Cs to every one of them. The company must be explicit that the primary resource for the business is the work force. The company must be clear that it will continually seek out what employees want and how to best provide it. A good book about doing this is *"The Baptist Health System Journey to Excellence,"* put together by Al Stubblefield. He has the same belief I do, employees first, customers second. Although I see them as both the same. Those who pay are customers. Those who get paid are customers. And the company itself is a customer. All expect and deserve the same thing."

I absentmindedly took another sip of the whisky. It wasn't so bad this time. I think my tongue was numb.

Angus continued. "As I said earlier, the company must make the first move, provide the 4 Cs to employees before it can expect the employees to provide great customer service. A sense of ownership is important. If the employees can have a real chunk of the company, one that is large enough to be meaningful, that does a lot. In addition, employees should have a legitimate say in goal setting and in creating the organization's vision, to as large an extent as the business has the courage to allow. The more, the better. Employees can act like owners if you allow them to participate in the process and enjoy a reasonable portion of the profits.

Look at it from a different angle. Every company has its nay-sayers. The complainers, the whiners, the people who can find fault with a free meal because it didn't come with chips. They can make the place miserable for everyone. Managers who lack courage or the ability to deal with these negative influences harm the company by keeping them around far too long. If employees owned the company, these folks would be thrown out on their ears. Loyal staff can exist only when they have enough say about what happens around them. How often does that happen? Not often. Managers don't make the tough decisions, hoping the problem employees will go away, or just as bad, criticizing the team as a group when the trouble is coming from just one or two.

This is where manager-employee relationships are as critical as employee-customer relationships. When managers and employees connect human-to-human, great things can happen. It is not an us-against-them mentality. The manager approaches an employee as a customer and the employee approaches the manager as a customer as well. There is trust, the most important currency in business. When trust is established, the manager can go to a complaining employee and say, 'Joe, all you're doing is complaining and depressing everyone's mood. Tell me what you want and if it fits into our team goal, you and I can figure out how to make it happen so everyone is better off. If it doesn't, you know we can't do it and you must accept that and move on.'"

I took another sip of whisky. It wasn't bad once you got used to it. "So," I said, "This is where knowing the employee's individual mission statements really pays off. You can talk to the trouble makers and find out exactly where the disconnect is between behavior and mission and work out things in a way that fulfills the team's vision and the person's mission."

"Brilliant, George. That's exactly right."

I held up my finger. "But there is more." Angus laughed. "Loyal staff know exactly what they get out of the job and it's the same as a loyal customer. They're going to get service from the organization in the form of support. They're going to get all the information they need to know what is going on and how they are contributing. And they are going to be totally respected in the form of having their personal mission supported and reflected in the team or organization's vision."

"I'm pleased George, but not surprised at how you're putting this together."

"You should write a book," I told him. "Anything else you want to tell me?" Angus smiled. He must be thinking that all he has done all day was tell me things. He probably thinks I'll forget most of it, but I won't.

"I probably haven't emphasized public displays of outcomes enough. May I discourse on those a bit?"

I nodded. A pleasant relaxation was settling into my bones.

"I believe that the system is accountable for the outcomes

and that individuals are accountable for the system. I also believe that the team is wiser than any individual on the team. I believe that there are such things as good mistakes. And I believe that transparency is the root of all good. If you agree, I want to talk about public outcomes and accountability."

"I agree. Press on."

"I shall. Loyal customers exist when an employee and the company treats them with the 4 Cs. Employees are loyal when the company and co-workers at every level treat them with the 4 Cs and, of course, when paying customers do too. These simple statements have significant implications."

Angus noticed my glass was empty. "Would you like a wee bit more?"

I smiled and answered, "Aye."

After pouring water and whisky into my glass and adding to his own, Angus continued.

"The significance lies in the customer, the employee and the company all acting as equal partners. What is good for one is good for all. What is bad for one is bad for all."

"Angus, I agree, but how does this happen? Who does what?"

"Now, we are talking about public outcomes and accountability, are we not?"

"Yes, and how the system is accountable, and everything is transparent and everything else we have talked about. How is this done? Where does it start?"

"Management declares it, then does it, then enables everyone else to do it and makes sure it continues to happen. Remember, I told you that the company has to begin the process of connecting human-to-human."

"So, at Superior Furniture, our CEO has to stand up and declare that we are going to be a service organization where everyone is a customer and we're going to focus on doing the 4 Cs. The CEO then does just that."

"Yes. Keep going."

"The CEO is going to define and proclaim her personal mission statement, make sure every workgroup has a vision and everyone has a personal mission statement that is shared with everyone. And everyone will define and declare how they will measure the 4 Cs…"

Angus stopped me. "How does that sound?"

"Totally different than anything I have ever seen or experienced."

Angus smiled. "Perhaps not. Think about that one-chair barbershop when you were young. Although unspoken, was everyone in the shop, customers and barber alike, aware of goals and expectations? And today when we went to the pub, would you say the same things were operating?"

"Sure. On a small scale, what we're talking about happens almost automatically."

"Aye. The values and roles in small operations are clear for all to see. You decide to go one place or another almost exclusively by how well they connect human-to-human, whether there is collaborating, if they contribute what you need, and by you feeling encouraged to give feedback, good and bad. You feel a sense of belonging there. You're a regular and enjoy that status. It's as if, you, the customer, are a valued member of a team that fulfills every quadrant of the four-part teaming model. It happens easily in a small business, but only with considerable effort in a large organization. That's why I put emphasis on transparency. That's important for the customer to see and it's also important for the employees to see."

Everything was clicking into place for me. There I sat in Angus McTavish's sitting room seemingly a million miles from Orlando, Florida. A week ago, I was floundering. This morning I wasn't much different. Now I was content. I was happy. I was anxious to get back to work. It was so simple. Every business operates for only one reason, to improve the lives of people, one way or another. It seems reasonable that if you improve the lives of the people within the business, you would increase the chances of improving the lives of the people outside the business; which means they will want to pay you money for whatever you are doing to improve their lives. And the chances of doing that should increase the more everyone within this system is treated as a customer.

But the larger the business, the more removed workers are from the buying customer. Rules are put in place by administrators. Employees begin to focus on themselves and their unconscious personal mission statements that have little or nothing to do with the vision of the organization. Hidden agendas flourish. Silos are created. Us against them mentality, whoever them is, is created and begins to guide behavior. Internal competition rewards the driven rather than the caring. Professionalism becomes a virtue. The bottom line is money, not adding value for all the people involved.

Why didn't I know this? But you can't focus so much on people. The bottom line is exactly that, the bottom line. If that isn't good, you have nothing. It's like a baseball team whose bottom line is the championship. They don't play to make everyone feel good, they play to win games and the World Series. That was the flaw in all that Angus was preaching about. Successful teams and successful organizations focus on results and design the process around getting those results. Okay, time out. Angus talked about success too, only putting more emphasis on the people part of the process. Highly functioning people was the process, a highly functioning, and thus a successful business was the outcome. All right. He focused on the process that leads to the outcome of a profitable business. What he talked about still made sense.

I suppose what he was actually talking about is as simple as the benefit of lubricating a machine. Just like you do what is best for your equipment; you do what is best for your employees. I just didn't have a clear idea of what that was. Business is still being run too much from the top down. We managed human interactions, so they fit the business, not necessarily the people. The massive diversity of the workplace was homogenized. I can see why Angus was so frustrated by service standards and scripts. Although they can be good tools when needed, most organizations simply create them and apply them like so much paint. The interactions may have looked good, but they covered up what should have been happening more naturally.

"Earth to Mr. Corbett. Come in, Mr. Corbett."

"I'm sorry."

"I fear my wee deoch en doris may have been too much."

"No, no. I'm fine. I was just thinking. Mulling over what we talked about today."

"Allow me to finish what I wanted to say about transparency and accountability. In small organizations, these two necessities are obvious. As an organization grows, what almost always happens is that policies and procedures, rules and standards, performance evaluations and the like are created, which become unintended barriers to what is important, great in-the-moment service for customers, employees and the company. What should be created are clear ways for everyone to identify their customers, define what their customers want, and how their customers can best be satisfied. This information, for everyone in the organization, becomes public and how well each employee is doing also is public. Transparency and accountability of the important things, not the artificial expectations most businesses fall victim to."

"Sounds like a good idea to me, and a whole lot of work."

"Ah, George. You're still thinking the old way. That somehow you can standardize what you want to happen and train everyone to do it."

"How else can it be done? You can't have anarchy. Can you?" Maybe Angus thought you could.

Angus had a one-word answer. "Stories."

I had a one-word reply. "Stories?"

"Aye. Much of what we did today, that made great sense to you, was stories. Agreed some of them were computer generated on the screen and some were real life observations, but all in all, I showed you, not taught you, what I wanted you to think about. The same should be done where you work and in every other business. Stories bring the concepts alive. Stories are examples of what can be done. Stories set the standard and are a library for future use. People incorporate stories in their own way and bring them forward in their own way when needed. And it can be as easy as pointing out someone who is doing it well. No need for extensive training. One picture is worth a thousand words. Tell me, which way is best to learn how to provide great service, a story or a list of things to do on a slide?"

"A story."

"And which interaction is more rewarding for the employee, connecting human-to-human in the moment or reciting a script?"

"Connecting human-to-human in the moment."

"And which is better for the organization, the employee using initiative in the moment to meet the customer's needs or reciting the company line?"

"Hold on there, Angus," I said. That particular question was not a slam dunk. But, of course, he didn't hold on.

"And which way is better to know how well satisfied the customer is, confirming so the customer is encouraged to complain at the moment of service or by formal customer surveys?"

I saw how he had tied things together. "When employees have the freedom to connect and contribute in the moment, and confirm satisfaction at the same time, I suppose that employees using their initiative is better than any company line can be."

"Right you are. One more thing."

"Of course."

"Think of the difference of publicizing how well an employee met a customer's need via in-the-moment connecting and contributing compared to publicizing how well the employee followed some programmed customer service standard. Which would be more rewarding?"

"The one where the employee showed initiative."

"Do you see what has happened? We've treated employees as simple cogs on a wheel. Give the employee responsibility and accountability to meet customers' needs, expectations and hopes, allow them the freedom to do that in the way that works best, make sure every employee has the same responsibilities and you have a wonderfully dynamic system that is self-reinforcing.

It goes back to my original idea that if everyone simply cared, it would all work very well. Every employee is aware of how he or she contributes to the big picture, contributes in a way that fulfills both the organization's vision and their personal mission statements, and, they're thanked all the time by their customers. You have loyal staff and loyal customers and a flourishing business."

I almost had it. "And how do you make this happen, again?"

"From the top. The CEO declares that employees are the customers of the business. Here, I'll just name the things the CEO declares in one way or another: the business is the customer of all employees, all employees have customers, all customers are to be treated with the 4 Cs, all service responsibilities and accountabilities are to be transparent, mistakes are to be accepted and used to improve the system, and everyone should define a personal mission statement and the organization will help them achieve it."

"No training?"

"Hardly any. Once leadership has declared what is to be, they begin to walk the talk. As successes are achieved, stories are told. As mistakes are made, more stories are told. Work unit visions are created by the work units. People are encouraged to let others know of their personal mission statements. Employees will become highly functional teams through fulfilling each of the four parts of the teaming model. Individual employees will learn and accept how their strengths contribute to the success of the work unit and what weaknesses the work unit will help them overcome."

"Sounds like Utopia. And a bit hard to imagine."

"Maybe not," Angus replied. "What's the difference between a one man barbershop and General Motors?"

"Is this a riddle?"

"No. What would you say is the major difference between a small organization and a giant one?"

I thought for a moment. "People? The number of employees?"

"Almost. It is not the number of people; it is the degree of connectedness between the people. There is significantly less in larger organizations. What most businesses do, as we have seen, is make human connections artificial instead of trying to enhance them. Remember the idea that we're all walking home together?"

"Yes."

"Picture a company of a thousand people all walking together. In reality, are they all the same or are they all different?"

"All different. Ah, companies try to make them the same."

"That they do. Instead, the company should make sure they're all walking to the same place and are connecting with each other along the way. Most people want to do that. You don't have to force them to."

"I can see that."

"All it takes is the courage to allow people to do what they want to do; connect, collaborate, contribute and confirm."

Notes

The company must have a vision that in one form or another engages everyone.

Transparency is the root of all good. Everyone should be measurably accountable to do the 4 Cs to everyone else.

It isn't company size that's the barrier, but impeded connections between people.

Employees should be cared for as well as machines.

Stories, not training.

Do everything possible to enable people to be people.

16

The Train from Dundee

I refused Angus' offer of a ride to the train. It was only eight blocks along mostly residential streets. Since I left my bags in a locker at the station, it was a pleasant walk. The setting sun lit the stone houses along the way with an amber glow. It was a bit chilly, but there was no wind. I passed the now familiar newsagent's which was closed and the bowling green, now empty.

The train from Dundee to Glasgow was the modern kind, side by side rows of high-backed seats. I had no more settled in when the snack cart came by. I was curious to see how this one would go, now that I knew about the 4 Cs. The woman pushed the cart wordlessly down the aisle. "Coffee, please," I said, and she stopped. She poured me a cup and handed it to me wordlessly. No human-to-human contact, but I did get my coffee. I said, "Thank you," but by that time she had moved on to the couple in the next row of seats.

The conductor came down the aisle not too much later. He said, "Ticket, sir," with just enough eye contact to make sure I was a sir rather than a ma'am. He looked at my pass, handed it back with a "Thank you, sir," but still no real eye contact, and moved on. He contributed by checking my pass and not throwing me off the train, but not much else. But did he have to? I wondered about that. How often should you do the 4 Cs? Do you do all four with every contact or is it more like the automated phone system where other needs take precedence? The conductor may not want to interrupt a passenger's trip by excessive conversation. Did I have any hopes that the conductor should meet? No. Maybe that's the idea. Some situations are just for a contribution while others should add connecting, collaborating, and confirming.

Then an idea occurred to me. What if I had initiated connecting human-to-human with the conductor? I've seen that a lot. The train conductor or the airplane attendant or the driver of the cab respond in kind to what the customer initiates. That made all the sense in the world. Perhaps with just a bit more eye contact, I might have told the conductor what a pleasure it had been travelling on the Scottish Rail system. He probably would have been gratified and we would have chatted a bit, both enjoying the contact and my confirming for him how good his company was. Even as simple an act as checking a pass could have benefited from the 4 Cs.

Then I wondered what I would have done if the conductor had been an employee of mine handing me a report rather than giving me my rail-pass back. How often have I just taken the report, said a perfunctory "Thanks," and gone about my business? In those moments eye contact would be enough to connect human-to-human, a more sincere appreciation would make a big difference for contributing from my end, and a simple question like "Do you have any additional thoughts about this?" might bring about a collaborative conversation to confirm the value of the task.

    I relaxed my head back on the seat. I was as content as I had been in a long time. Angus was right. The visit to him was the highlight of my trip to Scotland. The simple idea of connecting was so powerful. I no sooner had that thought than my mood sank, like an anchor disappearing into deep water. I was going home. To an empty house. To a job that no longer interested me. To a life I really didn't care about. A pleasant weekend on the Isle of Skye, a nice day with Professor, Doctor Angus F. McTavish, some new ideas about customer and staff satisfaction; did any of that make a difference? I thought about staying at the hotel near the airport that night and the flight home. I thought about arriving at my house and going to work. And I thought about sitting alone on the train at that moment. I pictured Susan, the housekeeper on Angus's computer. She had a mission, make a haven for guests that she could be proud of. What was my mission?

    I didn't have one. Only I knew that wasn't true. Everyone has a mission. What was mine? I knew that since Carol died, my life meant very little so whatever mission I had before I didn't have now. I sipped my coffee and pondered. Ideas and possibilities floated in and out of my awareness until a few sentences formed. Finally, I had something I could put into words. My mission was "Nothing is important so get through the day without any more pain." I didn't like it, but it made sense and felt right. No wonder I wasn't worth anything anywhere.

I sighed. It was decision time. I could continue going wherever it was I was headed, or I could create a new mission. If Susan really existed, maybe she could make me a haven. It was like she existed. Her message was real. If I wanted to be a happy employee, I had to identify my personal mission statement and start making it work. I would have to think about that.

My mood, that weight deep in the water, was beginning to be pulled to the surface. "We're all walking home together." I hadn't been walking anywhere and I sure hadn't been walking with anyone. Connecting human-to-human. That's what had been missing. When I lost Carol, I disconnected from everything.

I took a last sip of coffee and smiled. I was waxing philosophic, me, the only-the-facts-and-let's-keep-our-eyes-on-the-bottom-line guy. Of course, I did have wine at lunch and a wee dram of whisky.

How can we miss the human element so much? I was kicking myself for all the money I tossed at out-of-town experts and all the meetings and standards and lists that I and everybody else presented as gospel. You can't force somebody to be nice by putting words in their mouths, but that's exactly what we try to do.

Collaborate. Of course. Everyone is different. We see things differently. We must collaborate to make sure we know what must be done.

Contribute. How simple and true is that? Find out who

your customers are, what they want, then give it to them. Why wouldn't employees want to contribute? They wouldn't if they're dissatisfied customers themselves, that's why.

I stared out the window into the dark as I thought about dissatisfied employees. What value are they looking for? Cheapest price, best value/cost ratio, absolute best regardless of cost? I suppose some are looking for cheapest. If the job pays anything, they're desperate enough to take it. I would guess we have some of those. Best ratio? Most probably fit here: Enjoy the job and accept the pay and stay unless something better comes along. Probably the execs fall into only the best category. Most of us climb the power and dollar ladder in the guise of career advancement. What happened to people values?

I hated to admit it, but what happened to people values is management. We focused on the abstract "customer" and promulgated all sorts of interactions to "maximize the customer experience." We developed complex human resource departments to manage employee needs and they designed complex surveys to annually or semi-annually or quarterly determine staff satisfaction.

It's an old and sad story. Even Mr. Fezziwig, Ebenezer Scrooge's first boss, knew about caring for staff. Yet, he was discounted and run out of business. How hard is it to care about one another? Is there profit in caring? How is such a thing managed?

I smiled. Angus wasn't preaching anarchy, but close to it. He was promoting allowing people to be people as the best way to run a business. It was funny. Usually the ones most removed from actual customer contact make the decisions about what customer contact should look like. The intelligent, analytical, driven folks in corporate orchestrate human-to-human contact and what the correct behavior should be. It is so rare for a company to allow in-the-moment decisions about amends by staff that any company that does so is viewed as cutting edge or as taking extraordinary risks.

Don't most people want to be nice? Don't most people hate wasting their time? Don't most people want to be treated fairly? How hard can it be to get one human being to be nice to another human being? We have really screwed up. The wrong people are at the helm. Smart people are making bad decisions. Professionalism is eliminating humanism. Data determine decisions. Customers are becoming a commodity and so are employees.

I didn't like what I was thinking. I care about people. But it seems I cared more about the business. Then, when Carol died, I didn't care about anything. I was a mess, but somewhere in there was what was right for me and what was right for Superior Furniture.

Think this through. Why do I do anything? For me? For my family? For my ancestors? Descendants? Good of mankind? Superior Furniture? Its stockholders? Everything I do is eventually for people. What people? Me. I admit. I do things for me. And, my family. I do things for my friends and relatives. I do things for the good of others too.

I paused to notice where I was, on a train speeding to Glasgow. It was dark out. I was tired. The sunlit hills of the Isle of Skye were a lifetime away. I didn't need to figure it out. The value is in people. Living, breathing, human beings. I had to connect with them, collaborate, contribute, then confirm. I had to ask them to do the same with me. We had to ask each other about our visions and create one together. I had to ask and learn everyone's personal mission statement and help them achieve it. And ask them to do the same with me.

Angus McTavish, Ph.D., M.D., MBE, an extraordinary man from a small village in Dundee. George Corbett, BE, MBA, high-powered senior vice president of a growing furniture power in the American Southeast. Two savvy guys with mega-experience and a super computer. Two people who connected human-to-human, collaborated like nobody's business, contributed to one another, and confirmed how well it worked. But you know who did it better? Fiona, the newsagent. And Susan, the housekeeper.

Notes

Know your personal mission statement and change it as needed.

Buying patterns and similar data are useful, but we must remember that customers are humans, not abstract entities to be figured out, especially by management or administration.

When new employees join the organization, make sure they know the compelling task and know why they are valued members of the team.

Epilogue

The sun beat into the pavement like a hammer on an anvil. It was late afternoon and the temperature was 102 degrees. It was a hot day in the hottest month in central Florida. Thunderheads that had promised cooling rain kept their distance. I was standing outside my car waiting for the heat inside to dissipate so I could enter without fainting. I knew that within minutes the air-conditioning would make everything comfortable.

It had been a good day. In the few months since my trip to Scotland and most importantly Dundee, Angus's ideas had changed everything. I was anxious to hear the new quarterly satisfaction numbers due out tomorrow.

"George."

It was Henry waving for me to wait.

"George, hold on a sec. Impromptu meeting in the board room."

"What's that all about?"

"Numbers came out already. I don't know but I think there were a few surprises."

We turned back to the office, into cooled air, and up the stairs to the boardroom. Henry went back to his desk. I opened the boardroom door. Inside my four fellow VP's sat around the table looking glum and at the head, looking annoyed, was our CEO Helen. "I'm glad Henry was able to catch you. George, please sit down, I don't think this will take too long."

The room felt cold and not from the air-conditioning. It didn't make sense. As far as I could tell, the ideas I brought back had been well received and were working. I expected employee satisfaction to be way up, customer satisfaction to be high and our bottom line doing great. Obviously, something went wrong somewhere.

Randle, our CFO, spoke next. Before speaking, he took the time to look everyone in the eye. "We have the latest quarterly report and before going through the numbers, I thought it would be a good idea to list some of the changes we've recently made so we can better understand cause and effect. Mary, you wanted to start." He nodded to Mary who was sitting next to me. She stood up and went to a flip chart, which she turned to show my idea of how each department could create a vision to complement our new corporate vision statement.

"You all know our new improved vision statement, so I won't go into that, but I do want to summarize the model each of our stores and departments have been using to create work unit level visions, personal mission statements, and the team agreements." She went on to summarize what was on the flip chart.

Concepts, hopes, current state, dreams, etc.	Working phrases, words	Vision statement drafts
Concepts, hopes, current state, dreams, what enables you to end the day happy	Working phrases, words	Mission statement drafts

This was the simple template I introduced so each work unit could design its own vision statement by listing elements in the left-hand column they wanted included, then, by whatever voting method they wanted, to cull the ideas down to three or four, sometimes five concepts to include in their vision. Then, in the right column, write draft vision statements. The center column was used to store words or phrases that didn't work out at first but were good possibilities that should be saved. Each work unit did this for as long as it took to create a vision that made them proud to come to work. When that was done, the bottom part was used. Each employee went through a similar process individually to define his/her personal mission statement. When this was completed and then shared, team agreements were created so that everyone knew who was accountable for what to meet the team's vision and everyone's mission statement.

"I think this profoundly affected our success," Mary said.

"I'm next," Thomas said, standing up and going to the chart. He flipped over the page to reveal:

Connect
Collaborate
Contribute
Confirm

"These four words," he said, "simple, but complex, have made a tremendous difference. I must admit I thought 'connecting human-to-human' was sweet and quaint but lacked horsepower. But George kept insisting and I finally went to the extent of reading Martin Buber's *I and Thou* book and learned about I-it relationships. Buber said he couldn't explain it well so I certainly can't but connecting human-to-human is the most significant beginning I can think of for anything. Collaborating would seem like a no-brainer, but we salespeople, maybe more than most, have agendas we pursue rather than creating something with the customer in the moment. Contributing is probably the easiest element to understand, but it must be what the other desires. You must understand their frame of reference. Confirming, as George insists, has to be encouragement of feedback, an active seeking of new knowledge about the other person and what works for them." Thomas smiled and shook his head, "I am a changed man."

The mood in the room had certainly changed. I was beginning to relax.

"My turn." Monica replaced Thomas at the flip chart. She turned to her page.

Energy	Who
Caring	What
Openness	How

"We hire for column one and help them do column two. How simple is that? And it works." She sat down quickly. Monica was never one for public speaking.

"Now, me." Steve went to the chart and flipped over Monica's page to reveal:

Thank you

You're welcome

Steve smiled at Monica. "This is even simpler. It's not tough. It's easy to remember. Everyone can do it. And it works."

Helen stood up and went to the chart. She turned over the last page.

We're all walking home together.

"George, we've had the quarterly numbers for two days. I

don't know if this will ever happen again, especially since we don't plan to continue quarterly satisfaction reports, but the staff satisfaction numbers, those people who say they are extremely happy or very happy with their job at Superior furniture is 100%."

I had no idea what to say. I just looked at her. She continued. "We didn't do as well with customer satisfaction. Of those polled the percentage that said they were extremely happy or very happy with their service at Superior Furniture was 99%, and the percentage that was extremely happy was 84, that's a good loyalty number. The financial numbers are equally gratifying. We thought we'd surprise you with this meeting. You made the changes that got us where we are today."

I don't think I could have been more stunned, or happier.

Helen looked right at me. "Thank you, George."

I knew exactly what to say. "You're welcome."

Note to Managers

As you know, Angus insisted on keeping things informal, near anarchy if you ask me. I want to honor his concepts, yet at the same time I needed more structure, at least at the beginning. So, I put together some ideas and two tools you might want to try.

It's funny, I wanted to list the ten steps I took to get the great results we enjoy at Superior Furniture, but that would be making the mistake Angus taught me to avoid. You have to earn loyalty your own way, with everyone working together. So, here's a brief summary of what we did—but make sure you create what works best for your team.

First, I said a little and listened a lot, so did all the leaders and managers. We didn't assume anything. In small teams we discussed things like values, visions, missions, what we did well, what we didn't. What worked for us was to form small workgroups with specific responsibilities like how to help everyone develop a personal mission statement. One team came up with ideas to identify and define management responsibilities.

Second, we publicized all this work every way we could. We tried new ideas and made sure everyone knew what worked and what didn't. Not surprisingly, some of our failures brought out the creative juices of employees who often came up with better ideas.

By this time, we had creditability. The third thing we did was open the discussion of how we make sure we are doing the right thing and can continue to do the right thing. Eventually, we talked about peer accountability and lots of feedback and more importantly, support for those having difficulty.

In the end, we had everyone understanding that we all owned the work and the outcomes. Leaders couldn't make it happen, everyone had to be involved all the way. Leaders had to support and not control. Trust was huge, listening and responding was critical. But we did create some tools.

One of them is a survey you can take yourself or have your employees take. You can discuss the results, talk over how to improve what people do, that kind of thing. The other is a Skills Map, something you can put on a wall so everyone can see. People seem to love documenting how many skills they've acquired. It also helped some to decide that we were not a good fit for them.

The sample has names across the top. You may prefer names along the left side. My example uses an "X." You can use red dots, stars, anything colorful and interesting. Make sure the categories are the best ones for your needs, that the categories are well defined, and everyone knows and agrees with the definitions. Creating the skills map is a wonderful team building exercise and helps everyone focus on how to ensure customer and employee loyalty.

This 95% service idea; I think Angus meant that business is all about people. No matter if you're service or product, it's about people, employees, customers, everybody; their motivations, fears, dreams, hurdles, everything that makes us human. We must pay enlightened attention to the people side.

By the way, telling service stories works really well. My favorite is "My Day in Dundee."

George Corbett,
Orlando, Florida

Loyalty and Happiness Survey

This survey can be a self-survey or used to measure other individuals or a team. Check the box that best describes the person or team. It is designed to help determine current capacity to help create loyal customers and employees. The 1-5 scale is Never-Rarely-Sometimes-Often and Always.

This survey is about _____ Date _____

The identified person/team …	1	2	3	4	5	Thoughts Observations
1. Consistently follows the 4 Cs						
2. Provides service-information-respect to customers						
3. Treats all types of customers equally well						
4. Exhibits energy, caring and openness						
5. Has a personal/team mission statement						

6. Helps others fulfill their mission statements					
7. Creates and fulfills customers' hopes					
8. Ends most workdays happy					
9. Responds to a "virtual" customer					
10. Makes service a personal quest					

You can use other topics and change topics depending on your intent and specify each of the 4 Cs for measurement. This is a good way to identify what areas could use support. Discuss what barriers there are to scoring better and how the team members can help each other to do better. Immediate feedback from each customer, however, will always be the best way.

Skills Map

Skill/ Name	Sue	Tony	Myra	Tom
Connecting Human-to-Human	X	X	X	X
Collaborating	X	X	X	X
Contributing	X	X	X	X
Confirming	X	X		
Tells great service stories	X			X
Provides information		X	X	
Has a personal mission statement	X	X	X	
Knows other team members' personal mission statement		X	X	
Knows and fulfills company vision	X	X	X	X
Has a "virtual" customer	X	X		
Says "You're Welcome"	X	X	X	X

You can use any of the elements Angus and I talked about to create a skills map. The idea is to identify what you and your employees believe are the important components of customer and employee loyalty, define them and begin to ensure that everyone can contribute. Remember that the critical measure is how well employees and customers relate to one another, not scores on surveys.

Good luck! George

Note from Angus

My dear George;

Glad to hear of your success. Superior Furniture now really is superior. As you continue your journey of walking home together, keep in mind that earning loyalty is a two-way street. Of course, you must earn customer loyalty and earn employee loyalty. But employees must also earn your loyalty. They will sometimes forget that, or not know how.

Your job in leadership and management is to help employees do the 4 Cs with you as you do the 4 Cs with them. Confirm satisfaction a lot, everyday if you can and don't shoot the messenger when the news isn't what you want to hear!!!!!

Make sure they find out about your needs and satisfaction too. Be honest, open, transparent and they will be the same way.

Trust that constant use of the 4 Cs will teach you all you need to know as you and your company continually improve. Earning loyalty is an everyday activity, with a few honest mistakes occasionally, that will reinforce the value of the effort. Good luck my friend.

With warm personal regards,
   Angus

Index

A = F + h, 99
Accountability, 87, 88, 146, 153, 166, 170, 172
Accountable, 166
Agape love, 57
Amends, 99
Anxiety, 47
Aristotle, 111
Aristotle's Nicomachean Ethics, 14
Auto-attendant, 101
Automated telephone, 100

Baked potato, 79
Baptist Health System Journey to Excellence, book, 163
Barbershop, 136
Being open, 31
Berry, Leonard, 45, 111
Buber, Martin, 187

Caring, 31
Carlzon, Jan, 44
Clear goals, 146
Coal mine, 151
Collaborating, 65
Commission, 59
Compelling task, 128
Complaints, 87
Confirm, 78
Confirming satisfaction, 86

Connecting human-to-human, 51
Contributing, 65
Corbett's corollary, 138
Customer, def., 34, 36
Customer driven, 155
Customer loyalty, 47

D = f + H, 99
Delighting your customer, 55
Development Dimensions International, 95
Discovering the Soul of Service, book, 45, 111
Dissatisfied customers, 95
Duncan, publican, 84

Emotionally disconnected, 92
Employee feedback, 150
Energy, 30
Expectations, 97

F = E − R, 96
Fatal diagnosis, 17, 67
Feeling appreciated, 120
Feeling special, 42
First C, 51
FISH, video, 161
Fish market, 130
Focus on results, 169
Four-Part Teaming model, 128

196

Index 197

Fourth C, 78

H.E.A.T, 95
Hire for three qualities, 30
Hope, 43, 47
How to give your customers what they want, 35

I and Thou, book, 187
Ideal employee, 139
Indifference, 51
Indifference-love continuum, 113
Influence on the team, 128
It's a Dog's World, video, 161

Job satisfaction, 114

Key measure, 91
Kotter, John, 158

L.A.F.F:, 95
Labor department, 120
Lawn bowling, 28
Lencioni, Patrick, 111
Love, 56

Management, 118
Moments of truth, 44
Mr. Fezziwig, 180

New employees, 163
Newsagent, 29, 32, 33, 59, 63, 176, 182
Nordstrom, 87

Ownership, 137, 164

Personal mission statement, 147
Personal reward, 128
Pick-up line, 23
Professional, 108

Professionalism, 113, 181
Public display of customer satisfaction, 86
Public displays of outcomes, 165

Reality, 97
Relationship between customer and employee, 90
Rogers, Will, 59
Role models, 156

Scandinavian Airline Systems, 44
Scottish pubs, 83
Scripts, 20, 23, 24, 30, 37, 57, 88, 95, 159, 169
Scrooge, Ebenezer, 180
Second C, 64
See-feel-change, 158
Sense of membership, 128
Service culture, 159
Service enlightenment, 156
Service standards, 20, 37, 58, 157, 169
Service, information and respect, SIR, 65
Soccer game, 126
Standardization, 7, 77
Steps for superior service, 20
Stories, 170
Stubblefield, Al, 163
Susan, 141

Team building, 130
Teresa, Deanne and Harry, 120
Third C, 65
Training, 172
Transparency, 168
Traveler and the stone masons, 122
Trust, 164

Typical employee, 143

Value stream, 45, 76, 77, 80, 81, 86, 88, 136, 137
Vice president of happiness, 107
Virtual customer, 141, 153, 155, 157
Vision statements, 132, 144

Waiter, 60
Walking together, 12, 13, 173
What your customers want, 34
Who the customers are, 34
Williams, Rudy, 128

You're welcome, 81

About the Author

Bob Brown has been an independent performance consultant for over thirty-five years. He has also been a manager in small and large organizations, including overseeing service quality departments.

Bob has taught at undergraduate and graduate levels and worked with individuals, teams (including Olympic and professional athletic teams) and businesses to enhance performance.

His other business titles are:

The HST Model for Change
How to create and implement an organizational change plan that includes everyone from start to finish.

Lean Thinking 4.0
Using Lean Thinking tools and concepts to enhance people interactions. Introduces the Seven People Assets.

Transparent Management
Introduces Harnessing the Speed of Thought, Two Rules, the Organization-Individual Divide and further explains Rudy's Four-Part Teaming Model.

Mistake-Proofing Leadership (With Rudy Williams),
Using leadership "bundles" to ensure that the best outcomes are achieved.

The People Side of Lean Thinking
> *How to create a sustainable Lean culture which focuses on people and process.*

New Darwinian Laws Every Business Should Know (with Patrick Edmonds)
> *An unconventional look at the internal structure of business and how it should be changed.*

Bob lives in the Seattle area with his wife, a few cats and several species of backyard scavengers.

Contact Bob at books@collwisdom.com

Acknowledgments

Many of these ideas first saw the light of day in a collaborative learning group including Rudy Williams, Donna Smith, Eiliene Byrne, Jim Sapienza, Marlenna Peppler, Steve Stahl, and Bob Mecklenburg. Others who contributed to improving the concepts were Chris Covey, Georgia McKnight, and Shirley Miles-Watanabe. Jerri Bottomly taught me about the importance of agape and Rudy Williams taught me his Four-Part Teaming model. I also want to thank my editor, Gretchen Houser who was dedicated, timely, enthusiastic and critical in exactly the right balance.

Made in the USA
Columbia, SC
24 May 2020